ACTING

Ellis Jones

with a foreword
by Lord Attenborough

TEACH YOURSELF BOOKS

Long renowned as the authoritative source for self-guided learning – with more than 30 million copies sold worldwide – the *Teach Yourself* series includes over 200 titles in the fields of languages, crafts, hobbies, sports, and other leisure activities.

A catalogue entry for this title is available from The British Library.

Library of Congress Catalog Card Number: 98–67262

First published in UK 1998 by Hodder Headline Plc, 338 Euston Road, London, NW1 3BH.

First published in US 1998 by NTC Publishing Group
An imprint of NTC/Contemporary Publishing Company,
4255 West Touhy Avenue, Lincolnwood (Chicago), Illinois 60646-1975 U.S.A.

The 'Teach Yourself' name and logo are registered trade marks of Hodder & Stoughton Ltd. in the UK.

Typeset by Transet Limited, Coventry, England.
Printed in Great Britain for Hodder & Stoughton Educational, a division of Hodder Headline Plc, 338 Euston Road, London NW1 3BH by Cox & Wyman Ltd, Reading, Berkshire.

Impression number   10 9 8 7 6 5 4 3 2 1
Year   2002 2001 2000 1999 1998

Acknowledgements

In preparing this book I have had all kinds of help from many people and would particularly like to thank Nicholas Barter, the RADA Principal, our Chairman Lord Attenborough, Diana Hawkins, Francine Watson-Coleman, Robert Palmer, Kate Jones, Diane Worswick, Clare Hope, Peter Oyston, Nathan Hosner and Sarah Walton. Outside RADA, terrific help came from David Savile, Victoria Moss, Carolyn Lucas, Carol Fowler, Hugh Lovegrove; in the United States from Nancy and Lowell Swortzell, from Stephen Hollis, Patrick Quagliano and Sean Hewitt. Also Josh Randall for help with an obscure corner of American stage terminology and Harry Venning and 'The Stage' for kind permission for the reproduction on page 74. At home, remarkable patience has been shown by Suzy, Tom and Cressida.

CONTENTS

FOREWORD

Hardly a week passes without someone writing or buttonholing me to ask about acting as a career. The query often comes from would-be actors themselves but, increasingly, it comes from the parents of stage-struck young people who fear for their future in what is, undoubtedly, the most precarious of professions.

I try always to answer honestly, pointing out that the vast majority of actors are unemployed for long periods of time and that very, very few will ever make it to the top. I go on to say that, in my opinion, vocational training is vital and usually end by suggesting that the aspiring actor try to win a place at an established drama school.

There is, of course, a great deal more advice that I could and probably should give them . . . but that would fill a book.

Now, fortunately, such a book exists. The expert, lucid, inspiring and witty text which follows has been written by Ellis Jones, who is Vice Principal of RADA and has been in charge of acting tuition there since 1993. Prior to that Ellis freelanced as an actor and director for some 30 years.

His knowledge is, therefore, both encyclopaedic and very personal. He is a born teacher, gifted with the ability to explain the complicated and the esoteric without destroying any of their magic. But most importantly, although the book is crammed with many hard truths, his profound love of acting, both amateur and professional, is manifest on every page.

Lord Attenborough
Chairman, Royal Academy of Dramatic Art

Richard Attenborough, who grew up in Leicester, won a Leverhulme Scholarship in 1940, enabling him to study drama at RADA. Two years later, when he graduated from the Academy, he had already made his West End stage debut and appeared in Noel Coward's film In Which We Serve. *Since then he has become an internationally renowned actor/producer/director and an influential figure in the worlds of education and the arts. He has been RADA's Chairman since 1971.*

INTRODUCTION

At the Royal Academy of Dramatic Art in London every year we run a Summer School for four weeks during July and August; it's an 'open' course, in the sense that anyone is welcome, without needing to audition. Using the information supplied on the application forms, we divide the participants into groups according to their experience of acting, and thus we have some groups made up of professional actors seeking to 'refresh' their skills and others made up of dedicated amateurs. A favourite memory is of a married couple nearing their sixties, both keen life-long amateur actors, who bought each other a place on the RADA Summer School as a retirement present.

But the largest proportion of the participants falls into a different category – people who come because they're intrigued by acting, but aren't really sure where it might fit into their lives. As RADA's director of acting courses, I'm asked most frequently the following questions during the Summer School:

- Am I really good enough to be a professional? How do I find out? Do I really want to join such a notoriously precarious trade?
- If I decide to 'go for it' how do I set about finding training? What's the difference between a university drama department and a drama school?
- Is it possible to find work without going to drama school, without needing to join Equity (or any other actors' union)?
- If I do go to drama school, how do I then follow through and establish a career? How can I survive if there are big gaps between acting jobs?
- I love the experience of acting and would love to follow it as a hobby – what's the best way of going about that?

■ I love the idea of acting, and would love to use it in some
way other than being simply an actor. What other options
exist?

Before I joined RADA five years ago, I had navigated the freelance world
of acting, directing and writing for some 30 years, from earning a pound a
week as a student assistant stage manager in 'weekly rep', through years
of acting and directing in regional theatres in many parts of Britain, and
several periods of being a 'face' from television, with all the dubious and
elusive benefits such fleeting fame brings.

In this book I have tried to share some of this experience and also to share
some of the insights gathered from the near-vertical learning curve I've
been slithering about on since I became involved in one of the world's
greatest actor-training institutions, working alongside a truly remarkable
team of tutors, directors and administrators.

The answers to some of the above questions can't really be found in any
book – you will only ever find out if anything's worth doing once you've
actually tried to do it. But I have tried to provide a reasonably compact
'handbook' for those setting out. If you know Britain's Lake District you
will know the incomparable A. E. Wainwright's guides to fellwalking.
Now, I don't claim to compare my knowledge of the world of acting with
the late Mr. Wainwright's astounding knowledge of the Cumbrian
mountains, but I hope, as his wry and witty guides have added to many
people's enjoyment of nature, that this book affords some help across the
landscape of triumphs, disappointments, frustrations, hilarity and sheer
fun of that compulsive, irrational human instinct – the Need to Act.

1 | WHAT'S SO IMPORTANT ABOUT ACTING?

You can't get away from them: switch on your local radio station when you wake up in the morning and chances are the voice barking 'The Number One Music Mix' or whatever will have been trained some years before at a distinguished theatre school; you pick up the phone, stab blearily at the buttons, you misdial – and a mellifluous voice (clearly designed to play Lady Capulet) gently admonishes 'Sorry – the number you have dialled is unobtainable....'

Wherever you go, actors are practising their skills, booming advertisements at you from radio and television, making announcements – the actor who raises the British nation's temperature every night with the stirring cry 'NEWS AT TEN WITH TREVOR MACDONALD!' spent two years honing his verse-speaking at the Rose Bruford Academy. Dave Letterman and Oprah Winfrey served time as actors while assuming their present identities as icons of the American television scene.

But the main business of actors, of course, is acting out stories. The range of drama available today at the push of a button is breathtaking – from simplistic 'soaps' to highly sophisticated versions of classic literature. Every corner store sells or rents out portable packages of actors doing their job, so that if you're bored with one lot of actors on the television you can plug in a video and watch a fresh bunch.

Actors are part of the fabric of everyday life. The circulation of tabloid newspapers depends on the love-lives of television and movie stars almost as much on the sexual excursions of the British Royal Family. The British nation honours its great actors by making them knights, dames and even peers. If actors venture into the world of politics, their opinions are broadcast far and wide; some even use their acting skills to attain the highest of offices – would Ronald Reagan have made it to the White House without all those years before the movie cameras?

When Laurence Olivier died, a great ceremony took place in London at Westminster Abbey, with Michael Caine bearing a sword passed down from David Garrick, the great eighteenth-century actor-manager; when the Guyanese-born actor Norman Beaton died, three former presidents of his country were among the pallbearers at the funeral in Georgetown and in London a memorial service packed Southwark Cathedral.

None of this is new. When Garrick himself died in 1789, the funeral procession stretched from Westminster Abbey to St Paul's Cathedral. Because they've made us cry, or laugh, or thrilled or astonished or frightened us, we all have a personal investment in our favourite performers – and perhaps this is increased today by the fact that we get to know them in our own homes. When the news came of the death of Arthur Lowe, the star of the hugely popular British comedy series, *Dad's Army*, I remember feeling for weeks as though I'd lost a cherished uncle.

This quirk of human behaviour is endlessly fascinating. When we're children we all play 'make-believe' games: my six-year-old daughter will disappear for hours into a world of dinosaurs, ponies, babies, policemen, doctors, witches, trains, planes, spaceships, etc., – sustained improvization which may or may not include other children – and quite often a rich and complex storyline will develop with half-a-dozen apparently inanimate toys. When we're older, we love to be taken out of our lives into the worlds of completely imagined characters – several of my more intellectually sophisticated friends are simply unreachable by phone during transmission times of the BBC radio series *The Archers* and a senior arts administrator friend has her video programmed to supply a weekly update of *Brookside*, a highly charged British drama, every Sunday morning while she does the ironing. Doubtless *The Simpsons* in the United States and *Home and Away* in Australia have an equally distinguished following.

What is it about acting which makes it so indispensable? Some historians maintain that drama developed as part of human spiritual impulse, inextricably linked to the need to find meaning in an apparently chaotic cosmos. Allardyce Nicoll, in the classic theatre history book *World Drama*, maintained that 'the aura of religion pervades the whole of Greek drama'. My old tutor, the late great Stephen Joseph, took a more pragmatic view. He maintained that, at one of the Attic wine festivals back in the prehistoric mists, one of the Greeks, having taken in rather more than his fair share of that season's retsina, staggered up on to the barrel and made a speech, 'thus inventing the stage play…'

Whatever the truth of the matter, the early drama certainly had a social function; whole communities would attend the great festivals in ancient Greece and spend long hours absorbed in dynastic sagas, performed by actors in fantastical garb – masks topped with large hairpieces, flowing robes, high boots – it must all have looked a bit like a 1970s open-air rock concert.

But the content was heavy stuff, dealing with deep philosophy and high tragedy – and, seemingly, it meant a great deal to the public. Aristotle tried to analyze what the process was, and why it was so important. He identified the need for an audience to 'suspend its disbelief' and, in what he considered to be the finest plays – i.e. the Tragedies – to experience 'catharsis', that is a 'purgation' of the feelings of pity and fear. Ever since, academics have argued as to what exactly constitutes real catharsis and whether a teenage girl weeping helplessly at the end of *Sleepless in Seattle* is necessarily in a less elevated state than a university professor wiping his glasses after witnessing Dame Diana Rigg give her all as Medea.

Aristotle also attempted to define Comedy as 'an imitation of men worse than the average'. I don't think we need to spend time here debating definitions: however you slice it, most people love watching acting and, certainly in most Western countries, spend at least part of every day experiencing drama in some form – even if it's only a mini-drama intended to lend glamour to a jar of instant coffee.

For my money, Aristotle's 'suspension of disbelief' is only part of the enjoyment. Yes, a good actor will take you on a journey through an imaginary world and lead you through all the twists and turns of an ingenious plot; but part of the fun is to marvel at his skill, to admire the apparent ease with which he will share with you all the heartbreak of a divorce, say, or the agony of a bereavement when both you and he know that it's all fantasy, all the product of a professional scribe hacking away at a laptop wordprocessor like the one I'm using to write this book.

We in the business of training actors sweat for hours striving for 'psychological and emotional truth'; and yet people love watching 'Acting' for the sake of it – the sheer ballsy, rip-roaring ham of Olivier twitching his glorious death-throes as Richard Crookback on Bosworth field, of Burt Lancaster throbbing with evangelical fervour as he wrestles with his lectern in *Elmer Gantry*, of Anthony Hopkins's gleeful malevolance as he contemplates biting a chunk out of Jodie Foster in *Silence of the Lambs*. The thrill is in the risk the actor takes, soaring away on the edge of our disbelief, taking us into uncharted, scary areas of experience.

It's the 'purple passages', the outrageous blood and thunder – out-of-the-ordinary voice and gesture, preferably linked to spectacle of some sort – that punters have always paid for. In medieval times in England, the craft guilds staging the annual cycle of mystery plays would pay a professional player to act the Devil: clearly there was a market for special skills, someone who specialized in putting the wind up the citizenry.

What mattered in pre-cinema days was size – the ability to project in a large space. You needed a special magnetism, for instance, to hold your own in delivering long tragic soliloquies on a blustery day on the south bank of the River Thames in London, beneath the open sky of an afternoon in the 1590s, the Globe Theatre stuffed with up to 4,000 sweating, swearing, jostling bodies. Richard Burbage must have had magnetism in spades – why else would Shakespeare have written all those long speeches for him? Of course, not just Burbage: the glory of Shakespeare for actors is the wonderful range of crunchy parts for all the company. Try to imagine the 'suspension of disbelief' involved when a young male actor first set out to deliver Juliet's great speeches to this restless, *al fresco* London audience one afternoon in 1593.

Nowadays we demand silence and concentration from the audience, we create focus by darkening the theatre and throwing dramatic electric-powered light on the action; then it was all down to the actor, with his painted face and his wig, his farthingale and his skirts, to take the paying public into the highly charged world of a 14-year-old girl, bewitched and bewildered by teenage passion.

In the shifting, treacherous days of the sixteenth and seventeenth centuries, is it any wonder that governments sought to control the theatre, first by censorship and then by abolishing it? Up to 4,000 people in one place, under the spell of charismatic performers declaiming words with who-knows-what subversive intent? Actors and writers were altogether too potent a mix for a world being tugged apart by extremes of poverty and wealth, of worldly indulgence and religious bigotry.

In the dark days of the English Civil War and the Puritan-ruled Commonwealth, the professional craft of acting was banned in England; when the theatre re-established itself after the Restoration of the Monarchy in May 1660, it reflected a different world. The actors were still required to play tragedy, but the tragic muse had become stilted and academic, the dynamism of Shakespeare and his Jacobean successors had gone. The new age demanded glittering comedy, the actors flattering and satirizing the style and elegance of the post-Puritan court and its hangers-on.

The Restoration brought a new and irreversible dimension to the world of acting: enter the Professional Actress. It's intriguing to think of the backstage bitching as male actors' cross-dressing skills were made redundant. Did the actor who created Juliet and Cleopatra live long enough to see Nell Gwynne? It's unlikely but not entirely impossible; she first appeared at the Theatre Royal, Drury Lane less than 50 years after Shakespeare's death. One of the two actor-managers licensed by the king to produce plays after the Restoration, William Davenant, claimed to be Shakespeare's natural son.

The actors in the Restoration and early eighteenth-century years acted not so much in front of the audience as amongst them. Young blades would pay to sit on the stage alongside the performers – and thus have a very close-up view of the novel female actors. The 'asides' written into the scripts of the period were easily achieved, as the theatres were designed in a way that allowed intimate contact. Step onstage at the Georgian Theatre, Richmond, Yorkshire, to get a flavour of this. This theatre was actually built in the latter half of the eighteenth century, but the logistics are very akin to the Restoration stage: you feel it would be quite easy to shake hands with almost any member of the audience, even though the back row of the gallery in this (originally 400-seater) 'shoebox' is, in fact, a considerable distance away from the stage.

It was a tough world in which to survive, both literally and artistically. The plays were intricate and sophisticated, and must have succeeded, as many were written and many are still revived today. The demands on the actors were complex, requiring them to recite verse elegantly, deliver witty comments and asides, and often contribute songs and dances to the entertainment. The proximity of the audience had its dangers: there are records of audience disbelief being suspended to such an extent that actors playing villains were sometimes attacked by members of the public seeking vengeance on behalf of the heroine!

It was David Garrick who set out to make life easier for actors and, in so doing, pulled the professional theatre into a shape more recognizable to modern eyes. A man of sensational acting skill and considerable business acumen, he set out to regain control of the stage for the actors. As actor-manager of the Theatre Royal, Drury Lane in 1763 he removed audience seating from the stage. Garrick began to explore directional stage lighting, and to move the craft in the direction of 'naturalistic' storytelling.

And here we come to one of the most intriguing aspects of acting: what is 'naturalism'? Almost every age claims that at last the great actor of the time truly was able to 'hold as 'twere the mirror up to nature'. Garrick was hailed time and time again as a truly 'natural' actor. And yet, look at the paintings... Look at Garrick as Macbeth, striding the stage with his two daggers, look at him grimacing as Richard III. Did everyone behave in those days in what today we would call a theatrical manner? Or was it that such was the charisma of the man that he took his audiences so completely under his spell that they felt the world he created was completely natural even though it was, in fact, a contrivance?

Look back at the British films of only 40 years or so ago. Those clipped vowels, those staccato sentences used by Celia Johnson, Noel Coward, Leslie Howard and the like: did everyone talk like that then? Or was this a style which audiences expected people to use when they were in a play? Move on to the American 'method' films of the 1950s and 1960s. When Marlon Brando and Rod Steiger muttered at each other so magnetically in *On the Waterfront*, was it really 'naturalistic'? Or was it a heightened form of contrived drama which seemed effective with a camera just a few inches away?

What is certain is that the experience of watching acting is part of virtually everyone's lives, even in Eastern cultures where the mimic arts are traditionally more related to symbols – in mime itself, or dance, or ritual. Nowadays, largely because of film, video and television, the acting out of stories – be they never so fantastical in themselves, and may involve Harrison Ford or Sylvester Stallone plunging about in most improbable capers – is carried out in what is perceived to be naturalistic dialogue.

Acting involves an escape from now, from the stresses and pressures of reality. Many people want to experience creating that escape: either from deep psychological or emotional need, from a belief that life as an actor opens the way to glamour and adventure – or simply because it's a fun thing to do in your spare time.

Acting is both important and supremely unimportant. Its importance depends on how and when it's used. A great performance by a major actor in a great play by an important writer – Paul Scofield as King Lear, Dustin Hoffman as Willy Loman in *Death of a Salesman* – has significance in that the audience emerges with a deeper understanding of humanity, which may, just may, add to the sum of human happiness. Acting exercises in psychiatric or emotional therapy treatment are sometimes beneficial to the patient, and bring relief from suffering. A great comic performance may cheer you up for days, or longer – I grin every time I think of Alastair Sim in *The Magistrate*, 20-odd years ago. But no acting performance to my knowledge ever stopped a war, or prevented an epidemic. Because you felt deeply moved when you played St Joan in the sixth form and brought a distinct moistening to matron's fearsome eye ain't gonna change the price of mackerel, but you had a great time, and would love to do it over and over again.

The cruel fact is that you stand a much better chance of repeating the satisfying experience of acting if you stay in the world of the amateur. Finish your university degree, take that teaching diploma, earn a decent wage during the day and go out and thrill the locals in the church hall three or four times or more a year.

I hope, seriously, that most people reading this book will take that advice, or harness their thespian urges to social, medical or psychiatric use. I try not to encourage people to be professional actors. In pursuit of glory, or in pursuit of that elusive magical satisfaction from a part well played, or of glamour, or fame, too many lives are wasted. But for those afflicted with the vocational urge, I will try to point out the best choice of ways forward. For those who love the maid but choose to be her companion rather than her devoted spouse I will try to give some helpful pointers to a fruitful relationship.

What's so important about acting? What's so important to **you** about acting? Think carefully about what you want from it. Run a checklist:

What do I want acting to bring into my life?

- ■ Money?
- ■ Sex?
- ■ Fame?
- ■ Power over how I spend my time?
- ■ Sheer fulfilment – I won't feel a complete human being until I have committed myself to acting at the highest level, in great roles in the most distinguished company imaginable?
- ■ Fun: in the way some people play sports for fun, or paint pictures for fun, or play guitar for fun?

■ Interest; in an academic sense, an expansion of my knowledge as to how the world and the creatures in it function?

■ An interesting and varied career, with tough times and good, but with the good times far outweighing the bad?

I'll try to give pointers to help achieve all of the above objectives (not too much about sex, but read carefully, you might pick up a few tips...) Certainly, as regards the last of the above list, I can only note as objectively as possible that life for me in and around the world of acting has certainly many more highs than lows, otherwise this book would never have been written. It can bring all of these things, and it can bring poverty, grief, boredom, frustration, rejection, humiliation and, in the end, despair.

Quite a lot depends on where you're at in your own life. Some people harbour a sneaking feeling that they should at least try committing themselves to acting at some point in their life, on the basis that you don't know until you try. The short answer to that is if you haven't tried by a certain age then you probably don't really want to. Professional actors are constantly cornered in bars by people who 'of course, could have gone into the Business – everyone said I should but you know, parental pressure, the need to have a career, the need to eat ha ha...'

On the other hand, acting may well be something you need to get out of your system: there are examples of actors who, having made a distinctive mark on stage or screen, abandoned successful and glamourous lives to follow new careers they considered to be more satisfying, or more worthwhile. (Two of the great British names of the 1950s and 1960s, Brian Rix the celebrated farçeur, and Dirk Bogarde, the widely acclaimed film actor, moved on to become respectively a major figure in the world of mental health research and a distinguished novelist.) Others discover after a few years that acting isn't in fact as satisfying as they at first thought and move into writing, producing, directing, teaching or move off into a completely unrelated area.

One of the first lessons to be learned about acting is that, if it's really going to be effective – particularly onstage – an awful lot of work has to be done. True, there are gifted souls who can entertain and enchant from the cradle on, but ask any such person – Twiggy, for instance – if the really worthwhile acting work they've done just happens naturally, and prepare for a catalogue of hours and hours in rehearsal rooms, in gymnasiums, in classrooms. A phrase I repeat constantly to students at RADA is 'you are your instrument'. In other words, everyone knows that musicians need to practise, spending long hours each day pounding keyboards or plucking strings, but it's easy to forget that to play, for instance, Lady Macbeth on a big stage in front of a couple of thousand people requires a body and a voice with developed muscular strength, as well as physical and emotional stamina. I once sat alongside Judi Dench as she read a poem at a recital and realized that the vocal range employed in her wonderfully musical delivery was probably the spoken equivalent of Callas giving an aria by Verdi.

But make no mistake about it, acting is important at the time of delivery to only two people: the actor and the individual member of his or her audience. And the chances are that, however moved the audience member has been, he or she would have been equally moved had that part been played by any one of a dozen, maybe a hundred, other actors had they been cast instead.

For many people, acting is a passion, an obsession – but I venture to suggest that it's an obsession among a greater number of non-practitioners than practitioners. It's a great way to earn a living, if you can manage it, but when the chips are down **it's only acting**.

Suggested further reading

On Being an Actor by Simon Callow (Penguin, 1984)

Beginning by Kenneth Branagh (Chatto & Windus, 1989)

The Job of Acting by Clive Swift (Harrap, 1996)

Acting as a Business by Brian O'Neil (Heinemann, 1993)

Theatre (incorporating *Stagecoach*) a bi-monthly magazine published by Repertory Publishers Ltd

The Cambridge Guide to the Theatre (Cambridge University Press, 1995)

Brewer's Theatre (Cassell, 1994)

About Acting by Peter Barkworth (Secker & Warburg, 1980)

2 | WHAT DOES IT ALL MEAN?

Every craft has its jargon. Partly this is related to an atavistic, self-protective instinct expressed in the medieval guilds – the creation of a 'mystery' about the special skills of its members. It creates a feeling of being involved in 'something special', an exclusive activity beyond the reach of the common herd. It's also fun. My experience is that amateur practitioners take a special glee in using 'pro' jargon, and why not? If you've got a hobby, you should enjoy it to the full.

Sometimes jargon is useful for speed – it's much quicker for a director to say 'Bugger off OP, darling,' than 'Would you mind taking your exit into the stage wing opposite the prompt corner if it's not too much trouble, Daphne my love, if I've got your name right...?'

This 'darling' business – let's start with that. There is undoubtedly a tendency for male actors to call each other 'love' and to call actresses (and women in general, come to that) 'darling'; actresses tend to call everyone 'darling', period. It's probably less true nowadays among the younger more streetwise thesps, but it's still there, especially in the theatre. ('Luvee', I have to say, is not an expression I've ever heard anyone call anyone else, ever, in a theatre or a studio. Richard Attenborough has never used it, I have his personal assurance!) But to come back to 'darling'. I guess it's the same as chaps in more hairy-chested trades calling each other 'squire' or 'chief' – it offers a degree of flattery, implying that the person addressed is a bit special – and it does away with having to remember their name.

Remembering names can be a bit of a problem in a profession which has a high turnover of employment. If an actor is going through a busy freelance patch – spending odd days on television commercials, occasional one-hour bookings in voice-over studios, playing guest parts in single episodes of 'soaps' , spending some afternoons running workshops in a drama school, nipping down to a film studio to put in a couple of days on a movie, etc. – that actor will work with literally dozens of actors plus directors plus technicians plus dressers plus make-up people plus designers in the course of a single month, so the temptation to resort to an amiable catch-all name substitute is quite strong.

Incidentally, an actor friend of mine keeps a file of every person he either works with or meets in an acting context. This contains programmes of all the shows he's been in, cast-lists of television and radio programmes, notes of names and job titles of people he's met at interviews, social events, etc. It's a very good idea – an invaluable reference resource, allowing him to win brownie points in both social and professional encounters.

If you combine this with the tendencies for actors to be: (a) desperately insecure, in need of lashings of love and affection to justify their presumption in offering to get up and entertain, amaze and inform; and (b) imbued with an innate desire never to grow up and therefore to be treated and addressed as children, thus removing any need to take responsibility for anything other than – sometimes – having to learn lines, then you can see how the words 'darling' and 'love' became common currency.

'Darling' also has great versatility as a vehicle for expression. That long opening *dah* vowel can drip with syrupy affection, can smoulder with urgent sex, can sizzle with extreme spite and crackle with brittle fury. There was a generation of RADA-trained actors – pre-about 1969 – who had a wonderful way of declaiming 'Oh, but it's MA-AH-AH-VELLOUS DAHLING' about practically everything. Nowadays, it tends to be intoned in a sort of mid-Atlantic murmur – 'OK darling, see you 10:45 Joe Allen's' – but it's a jolly badge for the trade and I'd hate to see it disappear.

Those of us who grew up in the old traditions of repertory theatre tend to forget that young actors will stare open mouthed when you give simple directions like 'a gnat's further offstage', or 'come back after the ghost's walked' – so I've included at the end of this book a glossary of expressions the novice actor might encounter in theatre, bar, green room, club or studio.

I said in the introduction that I'm assuming some of the readers of this book will be the kind of people who might enrol on the RADA Summer School – i.e. intrigued by the world of the actor, but not necessarily knowing too much about it and keen to learn. If you want to pick the brains of people already at drama school, then the obvious places to go are the coffee bars, public houses, bars, etc. near the school. The sort of people who want to be actors tend to be the sort of people who like to swap stories, to feel loved in company and, sometimes, to drink. Oddly enough, drama students and actors love to talk about themselves, so for the price of a drink you could well buy several hours' worth of useful information.

To encounter working actors, again bars, plus certain clubs and restaurants are the obvious places. I must point out here that by no means all actors fit the roistering, boozy stereotype. Many are sober, hard working and are completely 'normal' in that they live ordered lives, stay for years with one partner, often have successful family lives, strive to keep up with mortgages, some are regular church-goers, attend PTA meetings and take their used glass jars to the bottle bank at weekends. But there are places where actors congregate socially, just as there are places where you will meet mainly lawyers, or doctors, or horse trainers, or dope dealers.

A good time to meet actors is often when they're in the full 'rush' of the only drug actors really go for – applause. For a couple of hours after finishing a show, most performers are in a 'high' state. The equipment has been firing on all cylinders – the voice, the body, the eyes, the teeth, the very soul – have been fully engaged in communicating and if the show's gone well, the actor is in sparkling form, delighted to chat with anyone, especially if they're discerning enough to have seen and enjoyed the performance.

(On the other hand, if the show's gone badly, the actor will be in depressed, nay suicidal, mood and is best avoided unless you want your ear bent for several hours on the iniquities of the director, the awfulness of the writing, the bovine stupidity of the audience, the parsimony of the management, etc., etc.)

If you're intrigued by the world of professional acting, and genuinely want to know more about it, you could certainly do worse than to get into conversation with people who have actually been doing the job that evening. Again, without wishing to reinforce stereotypes of actors as boozers, actors are as likely as office workers to want to go for a drink after work. Most of London's West End theatres have a public house or bar close to the stage door; a favourite with people working in the Shaftesbury Avenue theatres, for instance, is The White Horse in Soho, and for those working in the St Martin's Lane area, The Two Brewers in

Monmouth Street. Performers and crew working the theatres around the Strand and the Aldwych will often meet at The Peacock in Maiden Lane, or the Nell of Old Drury opposite the Theatre Royal. Probably the most famous 'Theatreland' bar is The Salisbury in St Martin's Lane.

Theatre-goers love to feel part of the theatre scene, and this will mean supplementing a night out at a West End play with a meal afterwards. There are, of course, restaurants in London where actors like to go after the play to entertain friends, agents, etc. Here are just a few: The Ivy, Monmouth Street, WC2; Joe Allen's, Exeter Street, WC2; Orso in Wellington Street, WC2; Luigi's also in Tavistock Street; Elena's 'Etoile' in Charlotte Street; 'Le Caprice' in St. James's. Of these, Joe Allen's is the least formal and least expensive: it's an as near-as-dammit reproduction of the famous New York original off-Broadway, serving New York-style burgers, pastas and the like. With all these restaurants you need to book if you want to indulge in after-show rubber-necking.

If you want to go with what used to be called the 'in-crowd', you could always 'go on somewhere' after the meal, for drinks and gossip in one of the clubs. That said, a club is a club, so you will need first to get to know a member who will be prepared to 'sign you in'. Clubs in London frequented by actors range from the clearly up-market (The Garrick) to the trendy (Groucho's and Soho House) to the cosy, such as 2 Brydges Place.

The thing to remember about clubs favouring members of a particular craft or profession is that the 'exclusive' air is cultivated for a purpose: it's where people 'talk shop' as equals, using a common language. If someone happens to be well known, a club is where he or she hide from the press and public, so clubs are definitely off-limits for autograph hunters.

In New York, theatre people congregate at The Players in Grammercy Park and in popular actors' haunts around Broadway include Eureka Joe's, the Friar's Club and Lamb's Club. Sardi's which is, of course, famous as the restaurant where many a first-night revel has either turned into an all-night debauch or quietly petered out, depending on the quality of the press reviews as they appear on television screens, does a special cut-rate meal on Wednesdays for actors between the matinee and evening showtimes. Not surprisingly, the place is packed to the rafters with Equity members. Off-off Broadway, the hottest place in town at the time of going to press is the Momba restaurant in Tribeca, which provides a useful day job for a struggling actor called Robert de Niro....

In California, simply get into conversation with the waiter at any restaurant....

I asked an Australian actor if there were specific hang-outs for thesps in Sydney and Melbourne and the response was 'Jeez, mate, any bar anywhere...'

Suggested further reading

The Cambridge Illustrated History of the Theatre (Cambridge University Press, 1994)

Contacts – published annually by *The Spotlight* (London)

The Actor's City Source Book (US) – published by Back Stage Books, NY, 1994

The Applause Guides to the Performing Arts – New York and California editions published by Applause Books

Also, the Glossary at the end of this book is essential reading.

3 | HOW TO ACT ONSTAGE

This book is *about* the world of acting: it doesn't set out to be a manual of instruction as to the best way of *learning to act*, in the way you might pick up, say, a manual on ballroom dancing, complete with diagrams of foot positions and little arrows showing you how to achieve a perfect quick-open-reverse-turn in the foxtrot. Acting is a subjective matter, there are many different way of telling a story and many different ways of moving an audience.

What do you need to succeed? Clearly, there are people who achieve fame and fortune without ever going near a drama school. Drama schools, as such, are a comparatively recent development – there were 'nurseries' for actors in London during the Restoration period in the late seventeenth century, but the modern schools emerged only during the early years of the twentieth century.

That said, I doubt if any working actor, be they struggling in fringe theatre or starring in Hollywood, hasn't had to go through some form of training, either by attending classes or studying hard the way more experienced artists achieve results. I've deliberately split this issue into two sections – acting onstage and acting in front of microphones and cameras. Most actors who work in the 'mechanical media' have some sort of background in theatre and, indeed, most actors, given the chance, like to work in all areas of expression, as the challenges are quite different. It is, however, much easier for an actor trained in theatre skills to adapt them for the microphone or the camera, than for an actor with only camera experience suddenly to get up and play King Lear at the Olivier Theatre.

If you want to work onstage, what do you need to be able to do? Briefly, you need to 'suspend the disbelief' of the audience so that they are convinced by your character and his or her situation; you can only do this if you are:

- able to be heard and understood by the audience;
- able to move, and conduct yourself generally, in a way appropriate to the character and the situation.

It's that simple, isn't it?

The problem is that all the characters we play are human beings. (Well, all right, you might occasionally play an alien, or an animal, but the chances are they'll have human, or at least humanoid, characteristics.) Human beings are complicated – you're a complicated phenomenon and so is everyone else you're likely to play be they imaginary characters or real historical figures.

The world of training for actors is beset with belief systems, largely through the proliferation of teachers following in the wake of Stanislavsky, especially in America. Constantin Stanislavsky was the Director of the Moscow Art Theatre at the turn of the nineteenth century, who worked with, amongst other playwrights, Anton Chekhov. Stanislavsky wrote a number of analyses of the acting process, intending to achieve the 'naturalism' and 'reality' required by contemporary writing. This coincided with the emergence of an international generation of writers treatising on matters social, domestic and political – Shaw, O'Neill, Ibsen, Granville-Barker, etc.

Stanislavsky's followers – especially in America – tended to concentrate on the emotional/mental state of a character. Matters of voice and movement tended to be regarded as secondary – and as the movie industry developed, it became possible to act very quietly, with the camera only really featuring your face, your voice being used, if necessary, 'as quiet as any mouse'. Hence a separate chapter on acting for the media.

But Stanislavsky is still a big influence in theatre school training, so let's come back to him later.

Being heard

First, let's look at the matter of **being heard**. Much use was made, at one time, of the expression 'projection': 'You must project, darling, you must reach Auntie Ethel in the back row.'

Modern voice teachers are more likely to tell you to 'be aware of the space'. The problem with thinking about 'projecting' your voice is that it easily leads to strain, to shouting and before you know where you are you've lost your voice. And if you go on doing it, you may well permanently damage your vocal equipment. So it's crucial to find a way of allowing your voice to carry without forcing it.

The thing to remember is that we are talking about muscle; muscle tissue will develop and strengthen if it is exercised naturally and regularly.

You also need to know something about how the process of speaking works, so that you can develop your equipment. Acting students study Voice, Phonetics, Speech and Dialect, often as related but separate subjects. Early in the course at RADA the students are given a fascinating illustrated lecture by an eminent laryngologist, complete with video pictures taken with a special camera of someone's vocal folds doing their work: and an explanation of how, for example, nodules can develop if the voice is misused.

All of these things can be learned about in books, but there ain't no substitute for practice. All I intend to do in this book is to give you some pointers as to how to start to use your voice properly and to urge you to (a) read the background material available in the books listed at the end of this chapter, and (b) take classes regularly with a recognized teacher.

The important starting point is to make sure the sound you make is supported with enough *breath*. Trying to make sound without breath is the same as trying to make a car engine start with neither petrol nor oil (the result, come to think of it, is not dissimilar, in terms of noise!) Also at the end of this chapter you will find a list of basic, daily exercises, intended to start you on the way to achieving the flexibility and range needed for, say, speaking Shakespeare's verse so that you can (a) be heard clearly in a fairly large space, and (b) create for the listener an awareness of both the sense and the beauty contained in the writing.

Movement

Now we come to **movement**. Again, there are many theories in this area regarding how actors can attain 'naturalism'. Most of us, the second we are asked to think about how we use our body, become appallingly self-conscious. A director said to me early in my career after I'd run through a speech, 'Very good, dear, what are you going to do about your arms?' Immediately my arms felt like windmill sails – inflexible, wooden, capable only of semaphore. To be told to do something – the most everyday thing, like picking up a cup 'naturally', is immediately to place a curse on the activity. The same thing happens when someone says 'just relax'; immediately you're aware of hypertension in every muscle.

The late Peggy Ramsay, the famous playwrights' agent, apparently would observe that you could always tell if an actor was truly 'in character' by looking at his or her feet. When I started my job at RADA I was approached at my first Management Council meeting by two very senior actor/board members. If I was going to be in charge of the training from now on what was I going to do about the fact that nowadays 'no young actors know how to stand'? In their day, they had classes in 'gesture' – what happened to teaching gesture? What was wrong with it? Why did it disappear?

Food for thought: you can sometimes find in libraries eighteenth-century and Victorian books prescribing how to indicate certain emotions onstage: 'To present Grief, lift the eyes to the Heavens, raise the right arm vertically, while striking the breast forcibly with the left hand…' Now, it's easy to mock this, but people *do* express emotions with their bodies and most of us gesture, in varying degrees, while we speak. Apparently something like 70 per cent of person-to-person communication is non-verbal. This must include the subtlest of 'body-language' (legs crossed away from – or towards – the person sitting beside you on the sofa) to the seemingly choreographed mass arm movements accompanying the chants on the terraces during a football game.

The problem for an actor is in recreating this without apparently thinking about it. We've already said that the human is a complex creature and various ways of achieving natural movement onstage have been developed by a range of interesting and distinguished analysts and teachers, such as F. M. Alexander, Rudolf Laban and Litz Pisk.

To be in control of your voice and your body to the same extent as a concert pianist controls the keys of his or her instrument must be the ideal to which any performer aspires. But that kind of control is achieved only after years of ongoing training and practice: one of the philosophies we try to follow at RADA is to train actors to learn and to keep learning.

So, once again, a book of this sort can only indicate the starting points: it's up to each individual to choose the path he or she finds most appropriate.

You have to start with a degree of fitness: acting is physically and emotionally demanding. You really can't take the audience on a journey of exploring the world of Lady Macbeth, for instance, unless you're fully alert, your vocal and physical equipment at the ready. So, before setting out on the detailed work, make sure the body is in good shape. This doesn't mean you should look like a Gladiator. Body building and 'fitness programmes' are notorious for creating tension, and denying the subtleness and flexibility an actor needs to express a range of characters and a range of emotions. Good general physical health – swimming is a good idea, regular walks, plenty of fresh air – is what you need; and then a programme of regular, **relevant** exercises and classes.

The range of physical disciplines available is, of course, endless, ranging from regimes intended to provide general poise and subtlety, such as the Alexander Technique, to specific skills, such as stage combat and classical mime, which will provide you with a broader range of wares to offer in the market place. For someone setting out as an actor, the important thing is to nurture a receptive, flexible instrument which can develop both generally and specifically. By this I mean that, should you have an inborn aptitude for say, song and dance, it would be a pity to limit yourself to just learning how to 'belt' songs and to tap-dance, at the expense of learning to explore the wonder of Shakespeare or the gritty joys of Restoration theatre.

With the list of voice exercises at the end of this chapter you will find some suggested physical activities, which, if engaged in regularly, will allow you to develop the kind of awareness and control you're going to need to feel confident as a performer.

Singing

Singing is an important element in the training of an actor. Actors at RADA, even those who claim to be 'tone deaf' are allocated a singing teacher, with whom they have a weekly one-to-one class, and all the students learn music rudiments and engage in regular choral singing. This has all kinds of benefits: as an actor you need a 'good ear', and developing musical awareness feeds your sensitivity to text written to be spoken, especially fine verse.

And the converse of my comment just now about 'musical' actors limiting their options applies equally to 'straight' actors who turn their noses up at musical comedy. Demarcation is still prevalent amongst British actors, although less so than it used to be; in America and elsewhere the term 'actor' embraces virtually all forms of live performer.

'Not being able to sing' is often a defence mechanism people put up against exposing themselves to possible ridicule – again, one of the paradoxes about the sort of people who tend to want to be actors is that, very often, they're basically shy. So having to get up, open the throat, concentrate on a melody line and share it with an audience is fantastic training – for many people, losing their terror of singing in public is a life-changing experience. During my time at RADA, I have watched lots of students discover new dimensions to their self-expression as a result of preparing for their Verse and Song presentations (which by the way, everyone has to do, be they never so 'tone deaf'.) One male student, an avowed non-singer when he first arrived, sang a splendid swash-buckling MacHeath in *The Beggar's Opera* in his final year and was promptly snapped up by the Cheek by Jowl Company for a world tour; a female student, only vaguely 'musical' when she arrived, discovered halfway through the second year that she had a breathtaking operatic vocal range and now makes a very satisfactory living as a professional singer as well as an actress.

Self-tuition in the field of singing is a tricky business: I would say you need at least some contact with a professional trainer to keep you on the right lines (this is, of course, true of all the skills, but especially so of singing; time and again 'natural' singers who suddenly make it big in the recording industry have to be rescued by professional trainers after they've been hammering their throats in public and suddenly can't produce any sound at all).

So again, use the 'grapevine' if you're in touch with the world of actors, or simply use the contact suggestions in this book to set up a relationship with a professional to monitor your singing exercises.

Acting

So, you've started working on your voice and your body – now what about the **acting**? I once showed the RADA timetable to a very experienced and distinguished actor. He nodded appreciatively at the range of voice and movement training in the curriculum and then suddenly jabbed a finger at 'Monday 3–6 p.m. ACTING'.

'What the Hell is an Acting Class?' He was genuinely perplexed. 'Surely either you can act or you can't! You can't *teach* someone to act!'

I explained that the classes are more properly called 'Acting Exercises', wherein students explore the ideas set out by Stanislavsky.

'Oh, all that stuff – The Method. Never touch it – in my day we learned to speak up and avoid the furniture.'

This is a fairly common attitude amongst older British actors. The beloved quote from Noel Coward – 'Just speak up and try to miss the furniture' – is often trotted out, as is the famous remark attributed to Laurence Olivier when faced with Dustin Hoffman's striving to use The Method to achieve 'real' terror in *Marathon Man* – 'Dear boy, why not try *acting* it?'

In fact, all Stanislavsky tried to do was to 'unpick' what effective actors do instinctively and to set out a process whereby a company of actors could achieve a collective 'truth' – i.e. whereby an audience's disbelief could be suspended more completely during the passage of a performance. The system he developed in Russia eventually crossed the Atlantic and was re-interpreted by the likes of Richard Boleslavsky, Lee Strasberg, Stella Adler and many other director-teachers. It was at Lee Strasberg's Actors' Studio that the term 'The Method' was coined, and came to be perceived as a way in which actors delved into their own emotional histories to stimulate something called 'emotional memory'. This could then be harnessed to inject the power of 'real' emotion into the make-believe situation in a play or film script.

Because the film and television industry was expanding rapidly at the same time as actors' studios were growing in New York and Los Angeles, many of the actors who developed their craft using The Method were absorbed into the screen world and, indeed, many remarkable performances were achieved – and still are – using these techniques. Paul Newman, Marilyn Monroe, Marlon Brando, Eli Wallach, Robert de Niro, Al Pacino, Dustin Hoffman – the list of actors trained in this way is long and impressive.

So what is it, this Method? Is it only useful for screen acting? Versions of the Stanislavsky system eventually re-crossed the Atlantic and are now taught in one form or another in most British drama schools. My view is that it's a good idea for actors to be aware of what are natural and instinctive processes and to have some form of control over them. There are dangers: use of 'emotional memory' can uncover psychological and emotional problems; too much 'navel-gazing' can create an incredibly selfish attitude, the antithesis of a sense of 'company'.

From the point of view of acting for the theatre, it's certainly true that actors concentrating hard on creating what they think is 'emotional truth' will often simply forget to speak up – and, in extreme cases, completely forget the basic disciplines of performance. (A young Eli Wallach apparently kept trying to interrupt Katherine Cornell during a soliloquy in Anthony and Cleopatra because he felt that his character would do so. She very understandably eventually slapped his face. Returning to his acting teacher to complain, Wallach was told by Lee Strasberg 'learn your cues'.)

This last anecdote sums up the great paradox at the heart of acting. There has to be 'truth' in order to suspend the disbelief of the audience, but there has also to be contrivance. We are always *performing*, be it onstage or on camera. The nature of that contrivance will differ according to the physical demands of the circumstances in which we perform, be they those of a basement theatre in Soho, an open-air amphitheatre or a sound-stage at Pinewood. There is undoubtedly a need to find the basic 'truth' in any of these circumstances, and elements of the Stanislavsky system can be useful.

The most helpful aspect of this approach, it seems to me, is in providing the actor with a checklist of questions, to use as a yardstick of how effectively you're telling your character's story. Depending on which disciple you read, Stanislavsky developed either nine or ten questions – for the purpose of a simple introduction, with the help of one of my teaching colleagues at RADA I enclose a distilled version of seven questions, which appear with the voice and movement exercises at the end of this chapter.

This is a purely subjective list: many teachers will disagree. (There are as many schisms amongst the followers of Stanislavsky as there are in the Protestant Church.) If you wish to explore this more thoroughly, then read the books listed and, if you're considering applying to drama school, find out which schools lay the most emphasis on this kind of work. At the time of writing, most schools include Stanislavskian elements in their training: amongst the London schools the Drama Centre perhaps lays the most emphasis on this kind of teaching. An interesting feature of the New York scene is that several of the famous Stanislavsky-based training studios are now affiliated to the New York University Tisch School of Performing Arts and provide modules for the undergraduate and graduate university drama courses.

A further word about 'emotional memory'. I recently watched again Tom Hanks's performance in the last sequence of *Forrest Gump*. Now, this is an emotional, some would say sentimental, film, but for my money Hanks creates a completely believable character. He manages to keep the scene where he talks to the grave of his dead wife well this side of mawkishness simply by concentrating hard on the situation as described in the script; it may well be that he tapped into some personal sadness in his own life as an aid to reaching the emotional territory in which he was working. But this is an actor in control, taking us into the moment in the character's story with pinpoint *accuracy*, not asking us to wallow in sentiment for its own sake. In other words, my guess is that Hanks, if stopped at the time and asked to run through the questions listed below, would have had a quick and ready answer for all them (which is not to say that he necessarily consciously went through them in preparing the scene – being the fine actor he is, they probably simply describe some of the processes he would go through instinctively).

To launch into recreating in your imagination all the detail of a harrowing or traumatic experience in your own life *may* be useful: it may also be self-indulgent and lead you into generalised self-pity, and into that most tempting of actor traps, that of *playing your opinion*. Just because a scene strikes you as being terribly sad and you've decided to tap into how you felt when your pet hamster died, it doesn't mean to say that your recollection of being upset when you were five years old is appropriate for the scene you are about to play. Also, the emotions experienced by you as a *reader* of a touching, well-written scene are not necessarily the same emotions as those being experienced by the characters in the situation. Too often, when I meet actors who wish to demonstrate their 'emotional range' at audition they seem to believe that this must include a display of 'real' tears. This happens a lot during the auditions RADA holds each spring in New York and, very often, I find the weeping applicant has some experience of attending Method workshops. My response is usually 'Please will you let me do the crying?' The audience has paid to be moved: the actor is there to serve the audience's emotional needs, not his own. Certainly sometimes tears are appropriate: but be sure they're the *character's* tears, not yours.

Note the phrase which came up a couple of paragraphs ago: emotional territory. By all means search your memory for real-life experiences which may provide a clue to the feelings required in a particular scene – but then use the questions to channel those feelings into the *imagined circumstances* of the play. This can happen in comedy as well as tragedy: an actor I once worked with in a repertoire season was called upon to play a scene in uncontrolled, hysterical laughter. He managed it brilliantly, night after night, and took the audience with him into several minutes of wonderful, hilarious comedy. When I congratulated him on this he said he'd been meaning to thank me for the inspiration. Explain, I demanded. Well, we were playing a long season and the management couldn't afford to carry understudies so had asked us all to learn some of the parts played by colleagues in case of illness. One of my 'cover' parts was Oberon in *A Midsummer Night's Dream*, which was played by an actor rather taller than me: at an early understudy rehearsal I had tried on Oberon's magnificent magic cloak, which on the appropriate actor looked superb. On me it looked like a wigwam. However, I rather fancied myself in it and struggled on, until I realized that the rest of the company were all speechless with giggling at how daft I looked... and this became the memory which supplied an endless source of mirth for my friend and, thus, indirectly contributed to the enjoyment of the audience later in the season. Emotional memory at its most useful!

The read-through

So: you're developing your voice, your body; you're concentrating on the emotional and psychological make-up of your character. Let's say you have been cast in a part of a decent size in a stage production. What happens now? Well, usually there's a '**read-through**', at which you meet the director, the production team and all the other actors. More often than not this will be in a rehearsal room, nowhere near the theatre in which you will eventually perform. You have coffee, you gossip, then down to business. The director may give a brief talk about the way she or he wants to approach the play. Then the reading: and first terror for the young actor. Some of the more experienced players seem to be giving complete performances already! Others, mercifully, seem only to be muttering their lines, giving a minimum of indication as to how they might eventually perform.

The point here is you need to have practised sight-reading. At every opportunity a would-be actor should pick up a script, a single speech, or a poem, and read it out loud. If your partner, flatmate or landlady objects to listening to you in the living-room, then hide away in your bedroom and chunter to a tape recorder. The most scary thing I observe amongst students is that many young people in today's video culture simply aren't used to reading the written word. And if you're going to act, you've got to be used to handling text. Get used to studying thoroughly and rapidly what the circumstances are which will inform how a particular line is said – is the character cold or hot, young or old, does he have an accent, is he likely to have a deep or a light voice, does he sound well-fed and contented, or starved and neurotic? If there's an accent involved, how do you achieve reproducing it? Hopefully you've got a good ear and a certain amount of natural mimicry – but you may well need to get hold of a tape or CD. (See the end of this chapter for sources.)

By no means is it necessary to produce a complete characterization at a read-through – many directors will prefer to develop the character with you in rehearsal. But, at the very least, you must make sense of the text at that first reading.

You must also display a sensitivity to the style in which the piece is written. A play written in a simple, direct 'dramatic' style – for instance, an Arthur Miller script – will clearly need a totally different approach to a comedy by Wilde or Coward. Again, think about the *circumstances* as revealed in the script. In *The Crucible*, for example, the characters are from a god-fearing, simple, rural culture. They spend much of their lives doing hard physical work, often outdoors. In *Private Lives* the characters live mostly indoors, drink lots of cocktails, engage in witty banter and go dancing quite a lot. In the first case these circumstances don't mean you immediately go into an earthy 'oo-ah' type mummerset and in the second you don't automatically launch into high-fallutin' lah-di-dah tones. But they do mean your voice will emerge differently if you think about the circumstances in which the sound is produced.

So, there you are, reading intelligently and clearly – you may not have all the i's dotted and the t's crossed, but if you've approached your initial readings of the play with an open mind and an attentive eye, the chances are that you're already well on the way to presenting a cogent, fully-realized character.

Rehearsal

And so into **rehearsal**. You may find that the director at first may want to explore the world of the play through games and improvizations. Don't be scared! Enjoy them, keep your antennae attuned to what they may add to your understanding of the piece – but keep going back to that text, read it at every opportunity. Not just your bits – work out what's going on in every part of the story which may have a bearing on your character. Above all, work out your character's *storyline*. (This will be even more important when we come to look at acting for camera.) Be clear in your mind as to the sequence of events in the story and just how it affects changes for the character. And remember that the character only encounters events as they happen *in terms of the time sequence in the play*. In other words, don't play Act 3 in Act 1. Just because the scullery maid becomes an executive for IBM in Act 3 doesn't mean she necessarily behaves differently from all other scullery maids in Act 1.

Of course, before going into your first rehearsal you will, having had the good sense to purchase this book, be familiar with some of the jargon listed in the Glossary and, thus, enter easily into the professional vernacular. 'Sorry, love, I've dried' will slip easily from your lips as though you'd 30 years in rep behind you.

Always be nice to the stage-management! They're the people who will make life easy for you. If, for instance, your character needs a particular 'personal prop' then ask for it in a friendly, not a bossy, way. Always be considerate to the person 'on the book'. Time was when virtually every actor would have been an ASM first, and learned the problems of prompting. A really good prompter can sense when an actor needs help, and will know the volume at which to throw in the missing word – loud enough for the actor to hear, but not so loud as to be distracting. If you've really dried and the prompter doesn't weigh in with the word, just say 'yes, please', or 'prompt, please' – **never** snap your fingers!

Never leave the area of the rehearsal room without permission from the stage or company manager; if the director 'clears' you to go home, make sure that you've had the next working day's 'call' from the stage-management – or that they've a phone number where they can contact you. The company manager is what the title says – he or she is there to make sure that the business of rehearsal and production runs smoothly and it's up to you as a member of the company to do all you can to help that process.

When you finally make it to the theatre for the technical rehearsal – 'the tech' as you will casually call it – it becomes even more important to collaborate with the stage-management. Their world suddenly fills up with light cues, sound cues, scenery which gets stuck, lorries which arrive late, costumes arriving minus a crucial bonnet, etc., etc. The last thing they need is a temperamental, or even worse, unreliable, actor. During the tech be prepared for a long day, especially if it's a technically complex show, like a musical. Good humoured, efficient actors are much appreciated by all the technicians involved and by the director. However, while it's important to remember that this is a day for the technical folk to get all their effects sorted out, it's also important for you to remember it's a last chance for you to master the technicalities of your contribution before the pressures of actual performance take over.

For instance, test the acoustic of the auditorium – make sure you know the degree of vocal power you're going to need. Check the sight-lines – once the set becomes real wood, metal, canvas, etc. and is no longer a taped 'mark-out' on the rehearsal-room floor, there are nearly always adjustments needed to various positions from which you'd assumed you were visible, only to find a large aspidistra cutting you off at shoulder height! If there's a moment depending on the efficient operation of a piece of equipment, or scenery (such as a door) then make sure you get the practice you need to ensure it happens properly every time: nobody's going to be pleased if ten minutes has to be added to 'the dress' while you're stuck onstage clutching a disconnected door handle in your elegantly gloved hand…

Observe the formalities of professional backstage organisation. Professional call-sheets (i.e., the details of forthcoming rehearsals) will list the actors' names as 'Mr' this or 'Miss' that. If you're lucky enough to have a stage-management who are able to supply individual calls during performance (usually over the intercom from the prompt corner) then it will be phrased as something like 'Miss Tutin, your call please' a page or so of script before your entrance is due. You *must* be in the theatre by the half-hour call before the show – in other words, **35** minutes before curtain up, as the 'half' means half-an-hour before the 'beginners' call, which happens when there are five minutes to go. The stage-management will also let you know when there are 15 minutes to beginners, and then five minutes. However, all such calls are a courtesy and do not detract from one of the basic rules of the trade, which is that *every actor is responsible for his or her own entrance*. If you're 'off' when you should be onstage, and your fellow actors are frantically improvising dialogue about the unreliability of trains nowadays, it simply won't do for you to complain that 'I didn't get my call'. The fact is that you're being paid to turn up onstage on time and to deliver a performance and that's your responsibility, no one else's.

A degree of formality in professional organization is very important: it's all too easy to slip into casual mode in the apparently relaxed atmosphere in which most of us like to work these days. The use of 'Mr' and 'Miss' by the stage-management may, at first, sound odd, but it reminds everyone that we're here do a professional job: it also makes it less embarrassing when professional discipline has to be introduced – for instance, if the company manager has to remind actors that repeated 'corpsing' (i.e. giggling during performance) is unacceptable behaviour.

Remember that it's the company manager's responsibility to ensure the paying audience see the show as booked by the management and as directed by the director; he/she is very much in charge of every thing that happens backstage and onstage from the minute the half-hour is called for the first dress rehearsal. From that point on, even the director has to ask the CSM's permission to go through the pass-door from the auditorium to talk to the actors or crew.

So there you are, a fledgling 'pro' ready for your debut. Don't forget to wish everyone 'Good Luck' – especially the person 'running the corner' (usually the deputy stage manager – DSM). By the way, the expression 'break a leg' is American so only use it if you're opening in the United States… And at the end of the show, don't forget to thank the stage-management for their help.

SUGGESTED DAILY VOICE EXERCISES

(Compiled with the help of Nathan Hosner, a graduate of both the RADA three-year Acting Diploma and the Acting Shakespeare courses, and approved by Robert Palmer, RADA's Senior Voice Tutor.)

1 It's probably a good idea to do your vocal exercises after your physical warm-up (see page 32). you don't have time to do a full physical work-out, then at least 'limber up' – move briskly about the room swinging your arms, generally loosen up the body with some stretches.

2 Get down on all fours, loosen through the spine with stretching movements. Watch carefully how cats do this and try to imitate!

3 Still on all-fours, take some deep in-breaths, focusing on moving the air into the back. Then release, with a deep, open-throated sigh.

4 Lie on your back, with a book or a firm cushion supporting your head. Pull up your knees to point upwards. Take a deep in-breath over a count of 5, then let it out with a sighing sound over a count of 10. Repeat, staying with a count of 5 for the in-breath, but increase the out-breath count to 15, then again to 20. Repeat this cycle several times.

5 Still on your back, part your teeth slightly and close your lips loosely over them. With throat relaxed and open, allow yourself to make a humming sound, bringing the hum forward on to the lips. Your facial 'mask' should start to tingle as you hum, making it buzzy and alert for action. Then run through a sequence of *moo, moh, mar, mai, mee* several times, making sure the sound is full and well forward in the mouth.

6 Sit up on a chair and use your fingers to loosen your facial muscles, massaging around your jaw and cheekbones. Without forcing, drop your jaw and allow yourself to make yawning movements, then work your muscles into a series of funny faces.

7 Starting with a low volume and building up as you progress, work through all the consonants in the alphabet, repeating each one twice on a rhythmic chant (e.g. bub-bub-bub-bub-bub-bub-bub-bub-bub-BAH!).

8 Stand up, stretch and recite to yourself a few of your favourite tongue-twisters – Peter Piper, She sells sea-shells, etc.

9 If you've time, now work through one of your audition speeches, imagining that you are performing for an audience.

SUGGESTED DAILY MOVEMENT EXERCISES

(Compiled by Francine Watson-Coleman, Senior Dance Tutor at RADA.)

Wake yourself up gently and easily – avoid jerky movements as this will create tension. Breathe regularly and fully in rhythm with the movements, allowing yourself to feel the expansion in the back and side of the ribs.

Repeat each activity several times, making sure you are fully aware of how it works and feels. You might enjoy developing your own simple sequences: give yourself variety by changing position, tempo, etc. You may wish to add music.

1 Loosen the joints and connect breath with action:
   – stand with feet comfortably astride, arms lifted above head, top of head held high;
   – swing forwards and down, arms, head, shoulders, upper back, waist – release knees until curled
   – rebound knees, bounce to swing up again – waist, upper back, shoulders, head, arms leading the return.

   Breathe *out* on the swing down, *in* on the swing up, keeping the neck relaxed and long.

2 Focus on your spine as centre, again with your head high, but held easily, without strain.
   – stand with feet slightly apart, arms relaxed
   – making one movement at a time, taking and releasing a full breath between each one.
   (a) Relax head forwards.
   (b) Relax shoulders forward, then the chest.
   (c) Relax forwards at waist, then hips, releasing back of knees until head and arms are 'hanging', towards the floor, breath easy and relaxed.
   (d) Return to standing, bringing hips over feet, waist over hips, chest over waist, shoulders dropped, relaxed over chest, head coming high, neck long.

3 Work the face through a range of expressions, not forgetting eyes and ears, ending in yawning movements, which stretch out into the whole body, including hands and feet.

4 Slowly roll the shoulders forwards – up towards the ears – draw them down from the bottom of the shoulder blades in the back, and release to hang free. Keep the spine up and lifted, the neck long, head free. *Breathe* with the action.

5 Standing, make a sequence of arm-swings across the body and to the side, forwards and backwards with an easy turn at the waist, then hips (feel the difference) and out around the body, wrapping the arms around in a spiral. Again keep the spine and neck lifted and free. *Breathe* with the action.

Repeat, using a weighty pendulum swing, contrasting this with the earlier, lighter sensation.

6 Stand with feet spread, lift your energy away from the floor.

(a) Stretch out as far away from your centre of balance as you can and clap hands. Then take them on as long a journey as you can before your next clap. (Do this to create a rhythm with your hand-claps. Vary the type and tempo of the rhythm each day, use different music, have fun.)

Cover as much of your personal space as you can, not forgetting along the floor, between your legs, behind you, etc., but don't strain.

(b) Standing in your space, let your eyes lead your body to take in your surroundings. Really look and see – pause to register shapes, colours. Don't forget to breathe!

To finish, lift your enegy level and sense of brightness by using springy feet and ankles to bounce the knees and stretch the body, easily, relaxed, keeping the spine lifted, the head high. Bounce from foot to foot, then let the hips come into play, then shoulders and head. Dance about and sing if you like, releasing the arms in the air – then gradually ease yourself back into stillness, finding a relaxed, focused centre.

If you are now going to do some voice work, repeat exercise no 2.

CREATING A CHARACTER AND TELLING A STORY – A CHECKLIST

(Compiled with the help of Jennie Buckman, Senior Acting Exercises Teacher at RADA.)

Depending on which book you read, Stanislavsky noted nine or ten key questions for an actor to ask her/himself when creating a role. Here is a version with seven questions only partly derived from Stanislavsky's list. There are, of course, many other versions.

1 Who am I? What are my outer characteristics and my inner ones? What happened in my life to develop them? Be specific.
2 Where am I? My behaviour will be conditioned by where I am in the world (national and/or regional characteristics, for example) whether I am indoors or outdoors, in a church or a bar, etc. Also by the sort of climate I am used to, or, again, more specifically what the weather is like at the moment in the story I am dealing with.
3 When is it? My behaviour will be conditioned by the period in which I live. (This will also decide the sort of clothes I wear which may, in turn, condition the way I move.) More specifically, my behaviour will be conditioned by the time of day (e.g. I will behave differently in the early morning than in mid-evening).
4 In the specific situation I am dealing with (i.e. in the play, or even more specifically the scene I am about to play) what do I want?
5 How do I try to achieve what I want?
6 What obstacles do I have to try to overcome? These may be inside you (e.g. Juliet's terror while summoning up the courage to drink Friar Laurence's potion) or outside (e.g. I am in love with this person but they are married and their spouse is in the room).
7 What effect do I want to make on the other character(s) I encounter in the story, and what effect do they have on me?

Suggested further reading

Voice and the Actor by Cicely Berry (Harrap, 1973)

The Right to Speak by Patsy Rodenberg (Methuen, 1983)

Voice and Speech in the Theatre by Clifford Turner (A & C Black, 1993)

An Actor Prepares by Constantin Stanislavsky (Methuen, 1980)

Building a Character by Constantin Stanislavsky (Methuen, 1979)

True and False (Heresy and Common Sense for the Actor) by David Mamet (Faber, 1998)

Sandford Meisner on Acting by Meisner and Longwell (Vintage, 1987)

The End of Acting by Richard Hornby (Applause, 1992)

Your Guide to the Alexander Technique by John Gray (Golancz, 1990)

Acting – The First Six Lessons by Richard Boleslavsky (Theatre Arts, 1933)

Respect for the Actor by Uta Hagen (Macmillan, 1973)

The Actor and his Body by Litz Pisk (Harrap, 1975)

Teach Yourself Alexander Technique by Richard Craze (Hodder & Stoughton, 1996)

Body Learning by Michael Gelb (Aurum, 1981)

Dialect tape sources

In a Manner of Speaking by J. C. Wells available from

BBC World Service
Bush House
London
WC2B 4PH
e-mail: worldservice.shop@BBC.co.uk

English Accents and Dialects by A. Hughes and P. Trudgill, book plus tape (Hodder & Stoughton)

Dialect Magazine by Roger Karshner and David A. Stern, book plus tapes (Dramaline Publications, 1994)

Accents for Actors, 1991 and *More Accents for Actors*, 1996 both by Carmen Lynne (Afora, London; available from Samuel French Ltd)

4 | HOW TO ACT FOR 'THE MEDIA'

If you're going to be an actor the chances are you will spend much of your working time in front of a camera and/or a microphone. Now, a lot of the acting most people see, especially on television, is of characters in 'everyday', 'real' situations behaving more or less like the folk they meet in the supermarkets or in a bar. So do you have to be a trained theatre actor to achieve success on screen?

I once saw the late, great, classical actor Sir Ralph Richardson being asked in a television interview to name his favourite film actor. Without a second's hesitation he said 'John Wayne – the voice, the presence – without doubt a very, very great actor.' Now, John Wayne, as far as I know, never went anywhere near a theatre school, from starting as a prop man to – some 30 or more years later – walking up to claim his Oscar for *True Grit*.

So the answer is no, not necessarily. But, in my experience, most people who choose acting as a professional craft really want to feel at ease wherever or however they are asked to perform, and, as we've already observed, if you come from Yorkshire and can learn the knack of speaking lines 'naturally' then you might thrive on the British soap *Emmerdale* for a while, but have a rude shock if your television fame earns you a job as Baron Bolinbroke in *Cinderella* pantomime at the Leeds Grand, and you lose your voice after two days.

If you are really going to experience the fun of acting, then you need to feel on top of your equipment; but to be in control of your voice and your body doesn't just mean creating the means of expression in a large auditorium. If you've got real command over your voice as an instrument, you can use it as a means of expressing a wide range of emotions and intentions whether you're 'projecting' for the stage, or 'containing' the volume for the microphones. But this doesn't just apply to the voice: you need to use your whole being as a means of expression, whatever the medium. The silent movie actress Louise Brooks, quoted in Kevin

Brownlow's *The Parade's Gone By*, says 'The great art of (acting in) films does not consist of descriptive movement of face and body, but in the movements of thought and soul transmitted in a kind of intense isolation.'

'Intense isolation' – it's a wonderful phrase, capturing the essence of so many of the great performances of cinema, radio and television. The great difference, it seems to me, between acting onstage and acting in a studio or on location is that acting for the media is, paradoxically, a one-to-one experience, although the aggregate audience reached may be many thousands or even millions more than will witness a theatre production. In the theatre, a collective experience takes place, as the actors and the audience set out on the play's journey together; the 'chemistry' between the audience and the company of actors is different every performance. Fellow professionals meeting in a bar or club after the show will invariably ask 'How did it go tonight?' This is most noticeable in comedy, particularly on tour: you can play to an audience who bellow hysterically at every line at Blackpool (or, say, Boston) on Saturday, and on Monday evening a packed house in Aberdeen (or perhaps Philadelphia) will sit through the same play in stony silence, while actors frantically dig their own graves by trying too hard.

Film, television and radio are not, in that sense, interactive, although, of course, 'interactive' drama of sorts is now achieved electronically on the Internet – but even this, for the most part, is one to one and you're likely to be interacting with a bloodless computer programme, not a group of live actors. The moment of drama as recorded by the camera and the microphone, once it has been processed by the editor, and released for transmission or distribution, is frozen for ever. In the theatre, the actor has a minute-to-minute contact with the experience of the audience and has, therefore, a degree of control. In the media, the control lies with the editor and the director – and ultimately, with the producer, who often reserves the right to over-ride the director as to the final shape of the product. The only exception to this is when you're a star with 'final cut approval' – in other words you've a contract which won't allow any scene you appear in to be released until you've seen and liked it, a situation which is only available to actors with major international clout. This is part of being regarded by film financiers as 'bankable', which we'll talk about later in this book. Needless to say, very few actors are in this position.

The most important thing for an actor working in any field is to have an understanding as to how he or she can best be seen and heard and how best to tell his or her character's story in the given circumstances. Let's make a checklist.

Being heard

Not as simple as it might appear. When I first started to work in television after several years' acting in theatres, I was struck by the fact that everyone seemed to be *muttering* their lines, if anything at a lower volume than in everyday life. There were highly sensitive microphones suspended a few inches above their heads, which twitched and swooped to pick up every breath, let alone the words. Being eager to learn, and not to betray my inexperience, when it came to my turn to speak I let the words trickle out of my mouth, using a minimum of energy.

When I saw the playback, my character barely featured, my lines being simply without colour or real meaning. So I set about watching the actors who really came across strongly on screen and tried to work out what they were doing which I wasn't. The answer, of course, was that they were *focused*. Their concentration on the moment, the situation, was total, but it was also a concentration on their equipment, including the voice – especially the voice. The character's intentions and feelings were being channelled through the voice, which gave it intensity rather than volume. Standing close to a major leading actor, I noticed that, as the floor-manager was counting down the seconds before 'action', the actor closed his eyes and took a long, deep breath. I was reminded of a tennis player about to deliver a crushing ace service. As soon as the camera started rolling, the actor was alert, totally alive – the words, the facial expressions, the bodily posture, the movement, all contributing to the moment in the story. The camera and microphone just had to record it. The point was that *the actor was doing the work*, not the camera or the mike, and he was working with *control and economy*.

This experience came back to me a couple of years ago, when I had a phone call from an ex-student who had just completed her first film-acting job. Like myself, she had fallen into the trap of underplaying. When she saw the 'rushes' of her scene, she realized that the actress she had been acting alongside – an established American star – had 'blown her away'. How had this happened? Did I know of any short courses for graduates concentrating on camera technique? The answer was yes, and, partly as a result of her phone call, training for camera-acting technique is now being rigorously developed and expanded at RADA as, of course, it is at most drama schools as the media culture continues to expand.

Just as when you're onstage you have to be aware of the geographical placing of the audience – whether you're playing in a proscenium arch or 'in the round' and thus adjust your performance accordingly – in the media you have to be aware of the disposition of the cameras and the mikes, because after all, they are effectively your audience. You need to know where the microphone is. The equipment may well be highly sensitive and the boom operator highly skilled, but you can still help him or her and yourself, by making sure that (a) your voice is clear and focused, and (b) your head is positioned in such a way that the sound can be picked up.

This kind of physical constraint, in all forms of acting, may sometimes seem to be hampering your creative flow; I mean, how can I express 'real' love and passion if I have to think about the angle of my head with regard to the microphone? The answer is that this sort of awareness has to become part of the creativity. It also underlines the co-operative nature of the work. Just as in the theatre you need to be aware of the pressures experienced by the stage-management, in the media you need to be aware of the problems facing the technicians. It's in their interest for you to look and sound right, and nobody is going to laugh if you ask the simple question 'Can, I be heard properly?' My favourite request from a 'sound man' came when I was recently playing the part of a medieval priest addressing his fellow villagers in the open air on location in Hungary. 'We're on a long shot, Ellis, and I can't get a boom or a pole in. The mike's in that bush over there, so just pitch it up a bit in that direction, will you, son?'

Being seen

Or rather, being seen to good effect. Just as you need to know how the mike is picking up your voice, you need to know how the camera is recording your image.

- Are you in close-up, mid-shot or long shot?
- How are you being 'framed'? Are you in profile, or is just the back of your head being seen? How much of you features in the picture?

■ Does the camera 'favour' you in this particular shot, or is another actor the focus? Once again, co-operation is important. When you're working with a single camera, you will often shoot the same sequence several times, first on a 'master' shot of the scene from the point of view of the audience, to give the idea of the physical setting, and then from the points of view of the different characters involved. So the director will shoot you saying a line from the point of view of the person you're addressing, and then turn the camera round and shoot the other person's reaction. This is called the reverse shot. For this, you need to play the line exactly as you did when the camera was on you and provide an eye-line for your fellow actor. It won't help if you've relaxed now you've done your close-up and start to fool about. Your fellow actor is now the one in focus and he or she needs your support.

■ What is my eye-line? In other words, where do I need to be looking? Alas, the eye-line the camera needs may be something other than what appears 'natural'. This is where your creative imagination is placed under demand. Above, I described a reverse shot: sometimes the physical setting you're working in won't allow the actor being addressed actually to be there. The space may be limited, for example, and there will be room only for the camera and the crew, so the character you're addressing may be a brick on the wall behind the camera, or a piece of cardboard held up by the third assistant. And the eye-line they give you may seem crazy, nothing like the angle you remember from the previous 'take', when the other actor was actually there. Trust them, they know what they're doing. Come the editing, your eyeline will be juxtaposed with the next image to make it *appear* absolutely 'natural'. It's all deception and artifice – or magic, depending on how you look at it.

Telling the story

This is very much your responsibility – another paradox, as I've already said that the control lies with the editor, director and producer. But they can only do their work well if your contribution is clearly stated. When you act in a stage play, you will almost certainly be taking part in 'linear' storytelling, with events happening in chronological sequence, thus allowing you to develop an emotional and intellectual progression as you take the audience with you on your character's journey. In film, and very often in television, you are likely to shoot out of sequence, sometimes playing, for example, your big emotional death scene from the final reel in the first few days of work, before you've had time even to get to know the people you're working with, and then going back the next day to play a jolly carefree scene when your character was two years younger. How do you cope?

■ First of all, you must read the entire script several times, no matter how small your particular part. You need to be aware of the function the author intends for your character in terms of the overall storyline.

■ You need then to examine the circumstances of each scene very carefully and in minute detail. This is where Stanislavsky-related questions come in handy: make sure you know how the character arrived at this moment – what happened between the last scene and this. If this is the first scene, scour the script for clues as to the character's history, then use those clues as building blocks in creating a biography for the character and establishing her or his state of mind at the start of the scene. At the *start* of the scene, mind. Always remember you are playing someone with a history, not necessarily a future. Sure, because you've read the script you know that your character plunges a bread knife between her lover's shoulder blades just after the final commercial break, but it's your job as an actor to discover the seeds in the background which create in her the potential for desperate violence, and then choose to what extent that potential is revealed (or obscured) as your storyline develops.

You may be lucky, and work with a director who will help you develop your character in rehearsal. But don't expect this as, increasingly, rehearsal time for drama in the media is dwindling. In the old days in Britain of *Play for Today* on BBC television, for instance, the work for the actors was structured much like putting on a play in the theatre. You turned up at the rehearsal rooms for several weeks' careful blocking, discussion of character, the social significance of the piece, etc. and then maybe spent two or three days in an elaborate studio, recording the play in sequence. This is now exceptional: you are far, far more likely to be shooting out of sequence on location, as you would for a feature film.

The reasons for this are, surprise, surprise, to do with money. Television studios are hugely expensive to build and cripplingly expensive to run. With the advent of high-quality, relatively inexpensive, digital equipment, it makes more sense to shoot on location, especially as the new equipment tends to be lightweight and very portable. Consequently, producers are planning budgets which allow for the product to be created almost instantly; the investment goes into shooting and editing, not into rehearsal. Even the most distinguished of directors may well simply not have sufficient time in his or her schedule to spend it exploring nuances of character with the actors – the director has to trust them to turn up with the lines thoroughly learned and ready to deliver an appropriate performance. The phrase 'turn up and turn over' is now commonplace amongst actors used to film and television work.

■ Learn to deal with the waiting and to keep your performance fresh. Another paradox: while it is usually cheaper for the director to shoot on location, it also often takes a lot longer to get stuff 'in the can'. You're at the mercy of the weather, of traffic, of the noise of aeroplanes, etc. Consequently, you the actor may turn up at 8 a.m. for costume and make-up. shoot one line of a scene at 9:30 and then wait in your caravan until 4:30 before you do the next one.

The actors, inevitably, end up 'killing time' together. This means you must (a) be good at Scrabble and have as wide a knowledge of card games as possible; (b) have a store of funny anecdotes either from your own life, or ones you've picked up on the grapevine about this great star or that megalomaniac director; and (c) be able to recreate instantly the intentions and the mood of the scene you are in the middle of filming. This, again, is where a checklist of questions is useful and, just as importantly, *remembering the answers you came up with when you started to shoot the sequence.* You might find it useful to jot down your choice of relevant points about the character's history and emotional circumstances in the margin of the script, to glance at as you hastily pull your wig back on, having been summoned by the third assistant just as you were about to wipe the Scrabble board clean by off-loading ANTEDILUVIANISM...

A final point about location shooting: watch your weight. Location catering is now a highly competitive industry and the range of free food on offer to film units is rocketing in quality. When you're sitting around on a rainy day, the temptation to ask for a second bacon-and-egg sandwich, or to go up for a third plate of the *foie gras en croûte* with sautéed potatoes and asparagus tips is heartbreaking. Fine, if it's your first job for four months and you're booked for only one or two days – go for it. But if you're in a serial or series being shot over several weeks or months, you're going to have to exercise self-discipline. Quite apart from the embarrassment of asking wardrobe to let out your costume waistline, you may find that, once the piece is edited together, your fluctuating shape plays havoc with continuity!

Working in front of microphones

One of the many paradoxes about the acting trade is that, while 'radio actors' are a threatened species, the total amount of work in general for actors skilled in front of microphones is probably greater than ever before.

While in North America radio drama as such all but disappeared as television gained ground in the 1950s and 1960s, in the United Kingdom the BBC Radio Repertory Company provided a haven for seasoned British pros whose faces the public never knew, but whose familiar voices in plays and series on the 'wireless' formed part of the nation's heritage and comfort. Once, when working at the Birmingham Repertory Theatre, I'd been in rehearsal for several weeks with a splendidly plummy-voiced elderly actor and had chortled through tea-breaks over his jolly reminiscences of 'the old days'. Suddenly, he slipped into a Midlands accent... 'Good Lord,' I thought, 'I've been taking tea with Jack Woolley...' (Jack Woolley, for the seriously culturally deprived, is one of the 'core' characters in *The Archers*, the world's longest-running radio soap-opera.)

In fact, even though the BBC has for some time been running down its Radio Drama Company, as the 'rep' is now called, the work for those lucky enough to be offered a place on it is richly satisfying and often quite lucrative. The 'jam' for actors in *The Archers*, for instance, is what are called transcription fees. This is the radio equivalent of overseas sales fees of television productions – the actors' royalties. *The Archers* is broadcast throughout the English-speaking world, and, although the late, lamented Philip Garston-Jones (he of the above anecdote) hardly earned in the Al Pacino bracket, he lived happily and comfortably in a beautiful house in the Cotswolds, his radio royalties forming the basis of quite a satisfactory income.

But the 'serious money' in this area of work is in the voice-over market. Think of how many times a day you hear voices peddling products over the radio and the television, or announcing events, trailing movies, etc. Listen carefully – you will often find the same voices being used over and over again. One of my friends is an actor highly skilled and well established in this field: in the evening's television watching, the family will chirp 'there's Andrew again!' often half-a-dozen times or more during commercial breaks.

My friend Andrew Burt is a member of a sort of unofficial 'flying squad' of actors who are in constant demand for this fastidious work. Companies requiring voice-overs often book studios and artists at short notice and for short periods of time – sometimes no more than half an hour. Consequently, the actors have to be available in easy distance of London's Soho – where many of the sound studios are – and prepared to turn up very quickly. Until mobile phones and pagers became commonplace, agents would issue their actors with 'bleepers', like hospital doctors on call.

For example, having been asked to get down to the recording studios by two o'clock, you will have to pick up a (usually completely new) script and make it 'come alive' instantly. Rehearsal, if there is any, is rapid, demanding flexibility and an instant response to suggestions by the director. If she or he requests 'a warmer sound, please', or 'it needs more underlying urgency', you can't ask to take the script home and think about it overnight!

To succeed in this kind of work you need another checklist.

- ■ Can you keep calm under pressure? This area of work is not a place for temperament – time is money, which is why the actors are comparatively highly paid. Artists who 'throw wobblies' are not likely to be asked again. The producers' money has the right to buy speed and efficiency, coupled with a talent for making a script instantly interesting, arresting or amusing.

■ Do you *enjoy* sight-reading? For some acting students, the phrase holds a kind of terror, because, alas, they come from a culture where the video rules and simply aren't used to the written word. One of my favourite television advertisements of recent years was the one in which a lady in New York asks a road-repair workman how she can get to Carnegie Hall. 'Lady, you gotta practise...'

I can't stress how important it is for every actor to arrive at the point where to pick up a piece of text and read it out loud is a joy, a chance to show off – if only to her/ himself. Get yourself a good-quality tape recorder and use it *every day.*

■ Once you're acquired your tape-machine, what weaknesses does it reveal? Record a short speech or poem and jot down during the playback:

  ■ All the words which are 'under-breathed' – words you thought you were saying clearly, but the tape shows you 'threw away', without investing them with thought or feeling. What consonants are slurred, fuzzed, or missing altogether?

  ■ Which are your habitual 'problem' consonants?

  ■ If you're working on an accent (either received pronunciation (RP) or a regional/foreign accent other than your own) which are the vowel sounds you need to work on?

  ■ Are you observing the punctuation of the text? Are you actually asking a question when there's a question mark? Are you using the commas, colons, semi-colons, etc., as 're-fuelling stations' for your breath supply? Having taken a decent intake of breath at the start of a long sentence, you can develop your technique so that you take in unobtrusive 'top-ups' along the way.

  ■ Are you able to 'scan' the text coming up even as the words in the sentence you are immediately dealing with are leaving your mouth? This sounds impossible, but it's a wonderful example of the flexibility of the human eye and brain. Even as one eye feeds in the words for the brain to interpret and pass on to the vocal department, the other can be searching the unfolding lines ahead, picking up on exclamation marks, question marks, etc. Trust me, this comes with practice...

■ How do the experts achieve results? Listen out on the radio for good sight-readers, on, say, the BBC's *Book at Bedtime*. Buy or borrow tapes of books and stories – there is a huge growth in the numbers available, as many people buy them for long car journeys. Given the notes under the above point, try to 'unpack' how the really experienced readers work. Any tape recorded by, for example, Miriam Margoyles, Martin Jarvis or Bernard Cribbins will repay lots of careful attention from a student of acting for microphones. American experts in the field include Richard Dreyfuss and Kerry Shale. These are just a few of the many actors whose work I admire in this field – make your own list of actor-readers you like and set about collecting examples of their work.

■ Who are you performing for? As in working with cameras, it's always good to remember the paradox that, although your audience out there may be numbered in millions, they are often experiencing your work on their own – maybe in the car, doing the ironing at home, or even virtually inside their own head, if they're listening on personal stereo headphones.

■ Are you using appropriate studio technique? As in the film or television studio, there are certain basic procedures which mark the experienced pro from the beginner.

    ■ Handle your script with a minimum of 'script rustle'. Hold it in the bottom right hand corner with your right hand, with your grip on the second page, leaving the top page free, ready to be turned when you reach the bottom line. Use your left hand to turn the page carefully, turning the script 'off mike' as you do so, while keeping your mouth in a constant relationship with the microphone. This applies when you're working standing up: if you're sitting at a table, it makes sense to unstaple the pages of the script and lay them flat on the table.

■ If you're recording a scene in a play or serial which demands your arrival into or departure from an ongoing scene, although approach and retreat can be simulated by the recording engineer, it's still helpful if an actor supposedly 'approaching' the scene actually starts by aiming his or her voice away from the mike, focusing in on the microphone as you get nearer to the person with whom you're playing the scene; similarly, you can aim your voice away from the mike as you leave the scene.

■ If the action requires you to shout, it helps the recording if your voice isn't aimed straight at the microphone. To avoid a 'blast', play 'across mike'.

■ Love scenes are great fun: the most sensuous 'kiss effect' can be gained by tenderly applying the lips to the back of your own hand an inch or two from the microphone. The biggest problem here is avoiding getting the giggles.

■ Have you read the script really carefully and marked in any tricky bits? I was once caught out while recording a serial for radio. On the first day I'd had very little to do, with only a few lines. Consequently I didn't take the script home overnight, thinking I would be able to manage with a cursory glance over the meagre part in the morning. As it happens, the director was worried about running out of time and so decided to go straight into recording on the second morning, with no rehearsal. I picked up the script – and found that the scene began with a four-page monologue by my character... and page three involved a chase through the forest and a fight! Taking a very deep breath and concentrating fit to burst, one eye racing ahead looking out for exclamation marks, the other feeding words through my racing brain to my mouth, somehow we got

> through it, the director liked it and with a 'Fine,
> thanks Ellis' moved on to the next scene while I
> dropped exhausted into a chair.

Working with microphones is great fun, but it's a precision craft and you should spend as much time as possible making sure you're ready to come up with the goods in very short order.

To sum up: most professional – and quite a few amateur – actors will increasingly work in the media. Just because cameras and microphones don't apparently require skills in projecting your performance it doesn't mean that the actor doesn't have to prepare every bit as much as for the stage.

Suggested further reading and viewing

The Actor and the Camera by Malcolm Taylor (A&C Black, 1994)

Secrets of Screen Acting by Patrick Tucker (Routledge, 1994)

Radio Acting by Alan Beck (A & C Black, 1997)

5 THE CREST OF A WAVE: YOUTH THEATRE

Although the regional professional repertory movement in Britain has been in severe decline in recent years, the youth theatre movement continues to flourish and, indeed, to expand all around the world.

What is a youth theatre? Usually, it's a group of teenagers or people slightly older – most groups have an upper age limit of about 22 – who meet on a regular basis to rehearse plays, take part in workshops and generally have fun in some sort of theatre-related way. Some groups are attached to professional theatres, some to thriving amateur theatres, some are drama clubs attached to schools and some exist purely in their own right.

Some youth theatres are run on a co-operative basis, with the group choosing events and productions by vote, some by professional 'youth drama leaders' employed by a local authority, others by specialist youth theatre directors attached to a regional professional theatre. Some are run on a voluntary basis by teachers or enthusiastic adult theatre buffs.

Are they simply clubs for teenage wannabee actors and nothing else? No, emphatically not. Of course, many professional actors started in youth theatres, but the vast majority of youth theatre members take part for the fun of it, have a great time for a few months or years and go on into a perfectly sane and respectable adult life, with just a residual whiff of the theatrical in the way they address board meetings, or their annual staff conference . . . .

Most youth theatres run programmes of workshops in various skills – mime, juggling, voice, dance, etc. and organize trips to productions at theatres in their area. Of course, they stage productions: sometimes only once a year, sometimes several, and everybody is expected to 'muck in' – although some groups organize backstage support for productions with a dedicated stage-management team, manned by those who love getting involved, but who don't want to act.

An exciting element in youth theatre is the opportunity to be involved in an expanding network of contacts, nationally and internationally. Some substantial sponsorship has appeared in recent years: large commercial organizations like to be seen to be linked with young, creative energy. Events like Barclays Young Stagers and BT National Connections give groups a focus for their activities and allow contacts with like-minded souls from other parts of the country. In Britain, the National Youth Theatre works hard to support and stimulate productions across the country and tries to set challenging standards of achievement by staging high-quality productions featuring young performers who have been invited to take part after a rigorous nationwide audition programme.

If I want to become a professional actor, will joining a youth theatre help me get into drama school? Not directly: in fact there are pluses and minuses. If you're in a youth theatre, you are in the same area of culture as drama training and you will probably make contacts with people in that field – either via the group leader, or through other members. If your group takes part in festivals, you will probably meet students studying drama in one form or another. Certain youth theatre groups are in touch with drama schools and help keen would-be actors prepare for drama school audition.

The down side is that, from the point of view of professional training, it's possible in youth theatre acting to get into bad habits. A lot of youth theatre production depends on high energy, high enthusiasm, and quite rightly so. To be in an auditorium with around 60 teenagers belting out the final chorus of *Bugsy Malone* is bracing stuff, a special experience. But the chances are that, in creating all that lovely noise, there hasn't been time in rehearsal to teach people how to make a big sound without risking damage to the vocal equipment. At worst, we find young people turning up at drama school with nodules on the vocal folds caused by several years' misuse. So take care.

A successful career in youth theatre can also be cruelly deceptive. At some of the festivals – in Britain the BT Connections Festival, for instance – you may find yourself performing on the Olivier stage, meeting afterwards the likes of Dame Judi Dench or Sir Ian McKellen, and thinking that you've arrived at stardom before you're 20. You then have to face the reality of competing with thousands of others to get into a good drama school, followed by all the struggle and disappointment that setting out to make a living in acting can bring.

Having said that, a certain youth theatre member was introduced to Sir Ian McKellen at the BT Connections Festival, went on to gain a place at the Central School of Speech and Drama, and within two years of graduating found himself co-starring with Sir Ian in *Peter Pan* at the Olivier Theatre . . . .

If you want to get involved in Youth Theatre, at the end of this book is a list of some organizations who will be able to give you details of the groups nearest to your home. If there isn't a group within easy reach and you feel there are enough like-minded souls in your area with sufficient determination to set up your own group, then turn to Chapter 6, where there are some suggestions you may find helpful.

6 | THE WORLD OF AMATEUR ACTING

The subtitle of this, as of the previous chapter, should be Acting for Fun. Not that Acting for Pay can't always be acting for fun as well; it should be, but there's a big difference between doing something that you really want to do and something you *have* to do because the bank manager, tax collector, landlord, etc. are queuing up and your credit card has just been refused at Safeway. Most professional actors will recognize that sinking feeling of turning up for a job you can only justify by muttering to yourself 'Think of the cash, old love, just grit your teeth and show the world you really *enjoy* dressing up as a camel....'

But if you really don't have a fateful sense of vocation – that unenviable state – then the theatre is there to be enjoyed in your spare time. There are thousands of terrific amateur theatre companies, many of which work to very high artistic standards. This is one area where comparisons really are invidious, and unnecessary. At the lower end of artistic achievement, I'd frankly far rather watch a display of 'bad' acting by an enthusiastic amateur cast than by an underpowered professional one. We've all sat and cringed with embarrassment and resented the price we've paid to watch pretentious and/or inept professional work. At the other end of the scale, there's a quality in fine amateur work which creates an experience different from high-standard professional performances. Not that professional work lacks integrity, it's just that amateur performers are coming from a different place. It has to do with the real meaning of the word 'amateur' – a lover. Not a spouse, a lover. Being married to someone – waking up with them every day, sharing meals, children, illness, overdrafts, etc. – is a different thing entirely from seeing someone for one or two evenings a week and the odd glorious weekend.

Elsewhere in this book we've looked at the tough choices you have to make if you really decide to try to make a living out of acting. If you're just not that sort of person, if you'd rather make your money out of doing a proper job but still find the world of acting intriguing and exciting, then seek out your local amateur company. If there isn't one, set one up. The world is full of people who are just a bit bored and want something to add interest and enjoyment to their lives: it really shouldn't be difficult to find fellow enthusiasts. Any way you slice it, theatre is a great hobby – at least great fun, at best wonderfully satisfying.

If you haven't discovered it already, essential reading is of course Michael Green's timeless classic, *The Art of Coarse Acting* (Samuel French, 1994). This richly funny review of the author's life as a dedicated and gloriously untalented actor is a joy, but as he points out, it intends no disrespect to the many thousands of talented amateur actors the world over.

What makes theatre such a rich element in anyone's social life is the fact that it is *shared*. One of the most influential professional touring companies in Britain has the brilliant title Shared Experience. You share with your fellow performers, your director and design/technical team the creative experience of bringing a text to life: this may, of course, also mean sharing experience with a writer or writers. You then, of course, go on to share the event you have created with an audience. In most amateur companies, 'demarcation' is blurred. If you can not only tear off a brilliant rendition of 'To Be or Not To Be', but are also a dab hand with a paintbrush and don't mind spending the weekend up a ladder, my guess is that most amateur companies will welcome you with open arms.

It's worth pointing out that some of the more established amateur theatre companies have links with the profession. Sometimes professional directors are employed: occasionally, professional actors are paid to play key roles. This happens in Britain, for instance, when the Mystery Plays are staged at York, usually under professional direction, usually with Jesus, God and the Devil played by pros, and all the other characters portrayed by local amateur performers. (This, of course, reflects the practice when the plays were first performed by the medieval trade guilds.) The Questors' Theatre at Ealing in London has an associated training programme which provides 'foundation' classes in theatre and many people go on from there to train full time at drama school. In the United States and Australia, many amateur theatre companies are linked to universities and thus have access to excellent theatre venues and to associated training courses.

The world of amateur theatre is large, varied and dynamic. Part of that dynamism is stimulated by *theatre festivals*, on a regional, local and international basis. The greatest festival of all is, of course, the Edinburgh Festival and many amateur companies – especially student companies – take productions there and perform 'on the Fringe'. Such is the pressure on finding venues in Edinburgh during the Festival (which takes place in August each year) that you need (a) to plan well in advance (i.e. up to a full year) and (b) to be sure that your company has the resources to absorb the costs of travel and accommodation, as well as of production. The reason why student companies are more likely to get involved in festivals than community-based theatre groups is simply that students are more likely to have the time available. Amateur actors who have commitments to careers in the real world may well have problems in this regard.

That said, there are festivals which are specifically organized for companies other than college drama groups; some dedicated amateur actors plan their holidays around them – in some cases this, presumably, assumes a family with more than one stage-struck member. You can find out about theatre festivals by contacting one of the 'umbrella' organizations listed at the back of this book.

How to set up an amateur theatre company

Time for another checklist.

Finding a venue

If there are only a few of you involved, you might hold at least your initial meetings and rehearsals at someone's home, assuming they have a reasonably large room available. But sooner or later you're going to need some sort of a hall. In smaller towns and villages this is often quite easy to find, providing you can negotiate time in the church hall or community centre with the scouts, the Women's Institute, etc. In cities it is sometimes more difficult, especially in central areas.

Cities like London and New York tend to be bursting with groups indulging in all kinds of activities from aerobics to politics – consequently anyone with a reasonable space to let is sitting on a goldmine. It's often cheaper to seek out a hall somewhere a little out of town or at least in the suburbs. Having said that, it's worth checking city venues controlled by local authorities or charities like the Salvation Army. If your group is genuinely a community-based initiative, or has some specific social 'hook' (like seeking to provide cultural activities for an ethnic minority, or has an educational or disability programme) you may well find that subsidized rates are available for room hire.

Far be it for me to encourage deception, but I have known actors in search of a rehearsal space suddenly to develop an earnest religious fervour and to start to attend services regularly, having discovered that their local church/synagogue/mosque has a general-purpose hall alongside it....

Choosing a play

Assuming you are getting together to perform established plays (as opposed to writing or devising your own) you then have to find scripts which will be practical to attempt in terms of the numbers of actors you have available, the balance of gender, the size of your design/lighting/ sound budget and facilities which may or may not be available at your chosen venue. Fortunately, some publishing companies often have usefully collated play-lists, supplying a synopsis of plot and a breakdown of casting requirements. Far and away the most comprehensive of these is published annually by Samuel French Ltd, with separate lists in Britain and America. The French's guide has dedicated lists of play titles categorized under cast sizes and gender breakdown, for example Plays with Seven Characters, 4m 3f, and then goes on to subdivide them into comedies, drama, etc. Spending a few pounds/dollars on the French's guide saves theatre directors hours thumbing furiously through scripts in the public library. (Samuel French Ltd also publishes quarterly updates as plays become available for amateur performance.)

If you're lucky enough to be near one of French's bookshops (addresses are listed at the end of this book) you are allowed to go in and browse through their reading copies. If not, they will happily send you reading copies through the post, on a loan basis.

Samuel French Ltd publishes most plays in the English language, in their special *French's Acting Editions* which can be either bought or hired in production 'sets' (i.e. with enough copies for cast, director and technical personnel). They also control performance licences for specific plays (see below) or will be able to tell you who does.

Finding funds

Initially, you may well have to find your set-up costs yourself, or club together with your fellow enthusiasts. Once you're organized, however, it's worth looking around for outside sources of funding or sponsorship. In Britain, regional arts associations have recently been encouraged by government to support amateur theatre initiatives, under the general slogan of Arts for Everyone. If you have an idea you think can be proved to be (a) of wide interest to your local/regional community, and/or (b) has potential to address in an entertaining way social or educational issues, you may well be able to attract support.

Attracting financial aid will probably be easier once you have built up a track record of achievement; but if you start with a really strong idea for a project, it won't do any harm to tout it around. Some arts boards will provide assistance to specific projects; others only support via regional umbrella amateur theatre organizations. Again, if an idea is strong enough, a regional arts board may supply a grant for an amateur group to employ a professional director.

Sponsorship is trickier. Unless you have especially strong links in the business community, commercial organizations are unlikely to come up with support for an idea for a one-off project from an unknown individual or a new group. Again, once you are established and are a familiar part of your local scene, you may well find that shops and businesses will provide either cash (or more likely) sponsorship 'in kind' in the way of paint, food, cheap furniture hire or even loan, in return for a prominent credit in your production programme.

If you are approaching organizations or firms for support, you must be able to demonstrate that you are hard-headed and business-like in your approach to the project. It's a good idea to create a concise project presentation document, containing:

- a *brief and clear* outline – name of play, synopsis of storyline, the play and the author's own track record in terms of previous successes, press reviews, etc.
- details of the venue and the dates you intend to perform
- details of your own credentials, and those of your group – other successful projects with which you have been associated with, etc.
- the target audience – who you hope to attract and over how many performances; why you think this particular idea has relevance and should attract interest

■ most important: a simple and credible *budget*: if you're not
used to drawing up budgets, it's easy enough to learn, and helps
you focus your own mind on just how practical your idea is.

To compile a budget, it's best to prepare it in the reverse order to the way
you will present it – in other words, work out your likely expenditure and
then fill in your projected income. If you are seeking financial support, the
key item under income, of course, is '*Other sources*'.

At the end of this chapter you will find a list of suggested budget items,
giving a typical (but by no means definitive) breakdown of production
expenditure against possible income.

At the end of this book you will find some details of amateur umbrella
organizations who will provide advice as to the best way of going about
raising funds, and of some public funding bodies.

Performance licences: scripts

Once you choose to present a play publicly, you are entering the world of
licences and copyright. If you're going to do a piece by Shakespeare or
any other long-dead writer, it's probably OK to go ahead, but you must
check that the script you are using is 'in the public domain'. Otherwise
you are bound by national and international copyright law. (In Europe, the
copyright period following an author's death has recently been extended
from 50 years to 70.)

In Britain at least, there is a difference between amateur and professional
performance rights. Amateur companies pay a flat fee per public
performance, professional companies are expected to pay a percentage
royalty on all tickets sold. French's will always advise you on the
licensing status of any particular script, in Britain or elsewhere in the
English-speaking world. If they don't control a particular script
themselves, they will give you the name of the agency which does.

Remember that photocopying a play not in the public domain is **illegal**.

Performance licences: venues

If you are intending to advertise your performance(s) to the public, you
must check the status of the hall or theatre you are performing in.
Anywhere open to the public is governed by complex and stringent
regulations to do with public health and safety. The owners of the venue
will advise you as to their status; if they have no public performance licence,

it may be possible to arrange one on a temporary basis. However, regulations are becoming more and more strict, so it is vital that you clear all the legal obligations before setting out to schedule and advertise your show.

The simplest way of checking the status of any particular venue is to contact the licensing office of your local city or town hall.

Remember, also, to contact the local *fire service* or fire department, as each production has to be cleared by the Fire Officer, who will make a visit, check your scenery for fire-proofing and will want you to demonstrate any use of naked flame in the show.

If the play involves using any kind of weapon, check with the local police. Even a pistol made only to fire 'blanks' will probably need a licence.

Marketing

One of the key impulses behind acting is doing it for an audience, so if you're going to put on plays, it makes sense to let people know you're doing it. This seems obvious, but it's amazing how little energy many theatres, amateur and professional, put into advertising what they're up to. Alan Ayckbourn once observed that many regional authorities seemed to enjoy a game called 'Hide the Theatre'. Sure, family and friends will come along, but the real challenge is whether or not you can hold the attention of total strangers.

If you haven't got the time to do it yourself, try to find someone prepared to take responsibility for publicizing the project. You need as many posters as you can afford, with a clear, striking image and preferably an eye-catching 'by-line' or slogan, backed up with as much press advertising as you can afford, plus strategically timed press copy, preferably with a picture.

Now, clearly, this is easier said than done – commercial organizations spend billions every year to achieve what I've just outlined. But given enthusiasm and imagination on your part, in my experience a local community will respond with goodwill – and it gets easier once you've established yourself as a purveyor of reliably good-quality productions. Local shops will display posters in windows (don't make them too big!), local printers may do special deals (and even help with the graphic design, if the idea grabs them). Bear in mind that the Press – local and national – is always desperate to fill space with interesting and entertaining copy. Think hard about finding a hook for a picture story. Depressing though feminist readers will find it, I'm afraid there are still many editors who will publish pictures featuring pretty women, however weak the story....

Establishing a company

Once you start to sell tickets, you become a business. If you are operating as a not-for-profit company, in which any surplus you make will be used for creating future projects, you may well qualify for charitable status. The laws on this, obviously, vary from country to country so it is wise to seek legal advice as to the best form in which to constitute your organization. As soon as you start to turn over money, there is the possibility of becoming involved with the taxation system, so, again, you should take advice before you start to offer your wares for sale. The amateur theatre organizations listed at the end of this book should be able to put you in touch with legal and/or financial consultants who specialize in this field.

Making yourself a movie star

Amateur acting is not, of course, confined to the stage. The Digital Revolution is galloping apace and near-professional-standard cameras and sound equipment are rapidly becoming available at prices accessible to groups or individuals able to find comparatively low sums of money. (At the time of writing, a near-broadcast standard digital video camera can be bought for under £3,000 ($4,900), and prices are falling.) You don't need a highly capitalised studio: 'location' filming can take place anywhere although, of course, you need to check with the local police and/or local residents if you are thinking of setting up your unit in a public place.

The biggest headache with using cameras and microphones on location is sound: just as you are about to deliver your declaration of deathless passion to the heroine, a plane flies overhead or a bus goes past. You're unlikely to be able to afford 'post-sync' facilities, which means you need to record sound as you go along – preferably with a separate microphone on a boom or 'fishpole'. So if you decide to venture into the world of movies and video, you're going to need access to some interesting but *quiet* locations. And start getting up early – the world is a quieter place first thing in the morning.

The next biggest problem is editing: if your final product is going to have 'shape' you'll need to be able to 'cut and paste' together your selection from a range of 'takes'. Some of the new video cameras have a certain amount of limited editing facility built in, but separate editing equipment is still relatively expensive. It is possible to hire equipment and a professional editor to help you use it. If you shop around, you will often find professional video and film editing companies who will do special rates for community projects.

A good idea is to make friends with students on a media-related technical production course: they often have access to good equipment, and, if they are on one of the many film and video courses which are now springing up all over the Western world, may well be in need of actors for their own projects.

But don't try to run before you can walk: as with professional training, remember it's usually easier to act in front of the media once you have experience onstage, and harder to adapt your acting to stage demands once you've got used to performing for a camera.

SUGGESTED STRUCTURE FOR AN AMATEUR THEATRE PRODUCTION BUDGET

Income

1 Ticket sales (You obviously have to try to predict the percentage of seats you are likely to sell. I'm sure I don't have to urge you to be *realistic* in this prediction!)
2 Subsidy (grants from Arts Council, local authorities, etc.)
3 Sponsorship and donations.
4 Sale of advertising space in programme.
5 Other sources.

Expenditure

Obviously, in a community-based company, a lot of time and materials may be supplied for nothing. But it's important to allow in advance for unforeseeable and unavoidable circumstances.

1 Physical production costs
■ set-building materials – wood, paint, etc.
■ costume-making materials and/or costume hire costs (a typically unavoidable hire may be, for instance, of wigs)
■ property-making materials or hire costs
■ construction equipment purchase or hire
■ workshop hire
■ furniture hire
■ lighting/sound equipment purchase or hire.

2 Professional fees. This may include a professional director, designer, or having to pay a professional to make, for instance, a particularly difficult prop. There may also be accountancy or legal fees.

3 Rehearsal room hire.

4 Travel/transportation costs.

5 Publicity and advertising costs, including printing and distribution.

6 Production photography.

7 Production running costs (e.g. laundry, cost of any food required by the production, etc.)

8 Administration costs: telephone, office space, postage, etc. Also subscriptions to relevant organizations, cost of printing tickets, etc.

9 Insurance.

10 Scripts – purchase or hire.

11 Royalities – author, also possibly performance rights fees on any music you may use.

12 Venue costs – hire, or if you have your own building, you may decide to amortize the annual costs of maintenance, heat and light, etc. over the budgets of several productions in the course of a year.

13 Contingency: some organizations set aside an additional 5 per cent or more of their projected total costs to cover unforeseen circumstances (e.g. suddenly having to hire extra equipment at short notice).

Useful publications

United Kingdom

Amateur Stage (monthly magazine).
Available from:
Platform Publications
83 George Street
London W1H 5PL
They also publish an annual Amateur Theatre directory.

The Arts Funding Handbook
Available from:
Hollis Directories Ltd
7 High Street
Teddington TW11 8EL

Plays & Players (monthly magazine)
Available from:
Northway House
1379 High Road
London N20 9LP

United States

Backstage (weekly newspaper)
Available from:
1515 Broadway
New York 10036
e-mail: http-://www.backstage.com

Producing Theatre by Donald C. Farber (Limelight Editions, NY, 1993)
Essential guide to American fund-raising, legal pitfalls, contrasts, etc.

Australia

Lowdown (bi-monthly magazine)
Available from:
11 Jeffcott St
North Adelaide SA 5006
Tel: (08) 8267 5111

7 | ACTING FOR CHILDREN

Acting for children – like its closely related and often overlapping activity, Acting in Education, which is dealt with in Chapter 8 – is something you really need to *want* to do. It's by no means an easy option: you can often fool an adult audience much more readily than a bunch of four to eight-year-olds. An audience of children won't necessarily boo you offstage if they think you're boring – they'll just find somewhere else to put their attention. On the other hand, if they like what you're doing, the reaction is terrific – noisy, exhilarating and intensely rewarding.

In some countries, children's theatre is regarded as a really important artform and there are heavily subsidized children's theatre companies, notably in the former communist bloc of Central Europe. In Britain there are important children's theatre companies in London, such as Unicorn, Theatre Centre and Polka. The tradition established at the Unicorn by Caryl Jenner in the 1960s is still vital and has fostered a dynamic range of playwriting and performing. The playwright and actor David Wood has established his own canon of specially written plays for children, many of which are produced by his own production company, Whirligig Productions. At the Stephen Joseph Theatre in Scarborough, the playwright and director Alan Ayckbourn has developed a special niche for children's work in his company's repertoire. Other writers have contributed significantly to the canon of plays available for children, such as David Wood, David Holman, Nona Shepphard and Adrian Mitchell.

In America, the Creative Arts Team at the Tisch Institute for the Performing Arts, New York University, provide a focus for children's theatre on an international scale. In Australia, a significant place for this type of work has developed through organizations like the Magpie Company and at the Carclew Young Performing Arts Centre in Adelaide.

The range of performance skills required in this form of theatre is often wider than those required by 'adult' productions. Children don't necessarily want to sit and listen to lengthy speeches developing an intellectual or philosophical concept; the performance may well need to satisfy eyes as well as ears. In other words, the actor may find her or his task much easier if she or he can draw on a physical and musical repertoire of abilities.

Puppetry, of course, is another field much loved by children. This ancient and rich form of storytelling, naturally closely related to the art of acting, is rarely taught as part of a drama school's main curriculum, at least in the anglophone world. If you have a passion to develop this skill, either as a complement to your main acting work or as a career activity, then I include at the end of this book some suggestions of organizations which should be able to point you in the right direction.

As with any form of professional acting, a course of training as an actor will stand you in good stead in whatever area you choose to specialize. Training in 'extra' specialist skills is something you can accumulate either in your spare time or once you have left college – most worthwhile acting training courses don't actually allow you much spare time.

You will, of course, learn elements of performance which are instantly useful – mime, for instance, is traditionally used in many performances for children and this is a skill which is given varying emphasis at different drama schools. If you are especially interested in going on to work in children's theatre, you should enquire carefully as to the range of skills training on offer at various academies. (See also Chapter 9.)

Many British performers with an interest in physical skills choose to take courses at the LeCoq school in Paris, so it is well worth exploring this possibility – see the contact list at the end of this book.

As I mentioned in the opening paragraph of this section, acting for children is often (and many people will say should be) indistinguishable from theatre in education, and thus several of the organizations listed at the back will be able to supply information about work in both the entertainment sector and projects linked to more specifically educational programmes.

Suggested further reading

International Guide to Children's Theatre and Educational Theatre by Lowell Swortzell (Greenwood Press, 1989) Essential reference guide.

Theatre for Children by David Wood and Janet Grant (Faber, 1997)

8 | **USING ACTING**

While it is true to say that the process of acting fascinates many people, it is also true to say that many people have no great desire necessarily to act themselves, or at least have far more sense than to try to base a career on expecting people to buy tickets to see them pretend to be someone else.

Such sensible people often have other vocations, ways in which they can see possibilities for making the world a better place by more practical, direct means, through education or through working in the fields of social work or healthcare. Other people simply want to get on with making a good living in industry or commerce. There is, of course, no reason at all why all such people shouldn't incorporate acting into their chosen walks of life.

Drama in education

This is a broad field and can be broken down into a number of areas:

■ acting in theatre companies specifically dedicated to bringing drama into schools and colleges

■ teaching drama as a subject within a curriculum

■ using drama to explore specific areas of other topics – the 'let's pretend' instinct in young people can be harnessed to unleash the imagination in the worlds of science, history, mathematics, learning languages, etc. For example, I know of one ingenious director who runs a brilliant workshop helping to explain the structure of English grammar.

N.B. As previously noted, the world of drama in education is, of course, related to the world of theatre for children and young people's theatre. The previous chapters on youth theatre and acting for children hopefully provide relevant information. There will obviously, therefore, be an element of overlap in the list of suggested contacts at the back of this book.

Acting professionally in Theatre In Education

Some years ago, many regional professional repertory companies ran educational programmes involving sending specially commissioned, specially cast productions out to schools and colleges in their area. Such plays often dealt with social or educational issues – race relations, literacy, etc., but also often existed purely to introduce young people to the kind of magic which led me to write, and you to read, this book.

Sadly, the decline of regional arts subsidy has led to this kind of work dwindling, at least in the United Kingdom. However, there are still some 40 companies in all producing dedicated work in this field, and there are signs of a revival. Some training schools and colleges now offer courses specifically in performing in an educational context.

The difficulty for TIE (Theatre In Education) producers is, very often, in finding the funds to mount and tour productions, as paying experienced actors Equity rates to perform in schools at the mercy of public educational funding is a circle difficult to square. There are some companies who balance their budgets by performing only in schools who have the financial resources to guarantee payment. My personal view of this is that if you have a commitment to using acting as a tool for education, it ill becomes the dawn of a new millennium to subscribe to a system denying a creative opportunity to the vast majority of youngsters in our society.

Some companies manage to survive on a commercial basis by charging schools fees sufficiently high to cover costs, but the number of schools with budgets adequate to hire in performers has, again, fallen drastically. However, as with many other forms of artistic endeavour, the concept of sponsorship is growing, and if you have a passion for this kind of work, and want to set up a dedicated company to produce it, it's well worth setting out your stall to demonstrate to businesses and trusts the clear benefits of being associated with adding new colour and excitement to the process of education.

It has to be said that some young actors seize on the idea of acting for schools as an easy option for gaining experience, of notching up professional credits for their Equity card. Well, yes, any performing experience is useful, but this kind of work requires and deserves special passion, special dedication and special skills. Unless you're in a place you want to be, performing material you believe in, the first people to spot your lack of commitment will be your young audience and the whole exercise will turn into a stressful event, with actors bellowing lines above a rising turmoil of at best, restless chatter, at worst outright hostility.

If you are interested in exploring the possibilities of work in this sector, at the end of this book there are names of education-based theatre companies and organizations.

Working as a teacher of drama in schools or colleges

Teaching drama is, of course, not the same thing as teaching acting. Acting as taught in good drama schools involves highly specialist trainers with technical knowledge of specific skills – voice, speech, Alexander Technique, period dance, etc. Teaching drama in schools will involve, of course, the teaching of rudimentary perfomance skills, but has much more to do with enriching students' lives through stimulating creativity as part of a co-operative group activity.

The benefits of drama as part of an educational process are easily demonstrable. Students who have difficulties in more academic reading-and-writing subjects often find release in, for instance, developing a devised play through group improvization, and the confidence thus gained goes on to help them improve their work across the board. As already mentioned, techniques developed as part of drama work can sometimes be applied to illuminating areas of other disciplines, such as History or Science. Theatre and its related activities are now perceived as vitally important elements in our culture, and subjects such as Theatre Studies and Media Studies now have a firmly established place among the advanced-level courses available in Britain and elsewhere.

This is a rich and complex field and too big a subject for the space available here. There is not space here to discuss at length the options available to those interested in pursuing a career in drama teaching, but a great deal of information is available elsewhere. Already mentioned in the suggested further reading list at the end of Chapter 7, Professor Lowell Swortzell's *International Guide to Children's Theatre and Educational Theatre* is the most exhaustive guide I know in this field, and will certainly provide you with details of the relevant organizations nearest to where you live. In addition, a list of useful contact addresses is included at the end of this book.

Teaching in drama schools

The whole question of training for acting is dealt with elsewhere in this book, mainly from the perspective of those wishing to be trained. For those who might wish to teach aspiring actors, the picture is sometimes confusing. Frequently, I receive letters and phone calls from actors – often very distinguished actors – who 'would love to come back and do some teaching at RADA, I feel I have so much experience I can pass on . . .' And indeed, often their experience is rich, but fruitful for the student actor only if it can actually be turned into useful components of the training. So while there is, of course, a place for 'master classes' by experienced practitioners, the real meat of any training must be the practical, specific nuts and bolts of technique. The greatest actor in the world may not necessarily be able to help to you to sort out why, for instance, you have a tendency to lisp slightly on certain consonants, or walk in a stiff and ungainly way. For this you need tutors who themselves have undertaken appropriate training.

Some drama school teachers choose their field of interest early in their careers and seek out an appropriate training. Many more work as practitioners – as dancers, actors, singers, etc. – and decide to move into teaching after some years' experience. This sometimes involves difficult decisions. In Britain, at least, most drama school teachers work on a freelance basis. In other words, it is unlikely that you will have a salaried, pensionable post such as you might have in a mainstream academic school or college. However, if you wish to teach acting in the United States or Australia, there are many more university courses geared specifically to craft teaching than in the United Kingdom, and, consequently, more resident faculty teaching staff.

In Britain, the greater part of teaching work in drama schools is often organized on a term-by-term, ad hoc basis. So in order to survive, you need to build up a portfolio of teaching commitments, perhaps amongst a number of schools, perhaps also involving advertising for private pupils, whom you may have to teach at your home, or else hire a teaching space.

This can create difficulties if you wish to continue to be available for performing. A drama school course director will almost certainly need you to commit to so many hours per week for at least one term – between 10 and 12 weeks. He or she may only be able to offer you, say, two or three afternoons per week – perhaps nine hours' work. Obviously this won't be enough to live on; so you have to be prepared to spread your net quite widely to build up a range of work opportunities. This may mean that you will be faced with the choice of taking, say, a week's television acting work or ten weeks of teaching one day per week. Now, most course directors are sympathetic and will try to schedule around your availability, but if the television job turns into, say, three weeks' continuous work, then you have to start casting about for a deputy, and the quality of the students' learning process starts to be threatened.

My usual advice to performers intending to shift the emphasis of their work to teaching is to take themselves off the market as actors until such time as they have sorted out a teaching agenda. This will, in most cases, involve re-training in some form and, of course, some networking amongst contacts in the drama training world. Once you have established a reasonably satisfying portfolio of regular teaching jobs, you can then tell your agent only to put you up for acting jobs which fit around your teaching schedule.

Think hard before you set out on this path. Here is a checklist.

1 What, exactly, do you want to teach? (The more specific you can be, the easier to move on to the next step.)

2 Have you honestly examined what teaching your chosen subject involves? Can you plan a whole term's work? For example, have you in place yardsticks by which you can measure students' progress?

3 Have you found out about specific qualifications which you can add to your CV and thus add to your credibility as a teacher? For example, a diploma from a recognized academy in voice teaching or a fight director's certificate?

4 Have you saved up money to help you survive while you take yourself off the market as an actor, dancer, or whatever is your usual source of income?

It would appear, at the time of writing, that there might be an expanding market place for teachers of acting, certainly in Britain, where *The Stage* newspaper carries several weekly pages of advertisements for drama schools. In New York, *Back Stage* carries even more and, from time to time, runs substantial special supplements on training opportunities.

However, in both publications the number of advertisements for students for the schools does not seem to be reflected in the number of advertisements for teaching jobs. Many of these schools are quite new, so perhaps if they establish themselves then a need for replacement staff will develop. Be that as it may, as a course director of a school requiring demonstrably well-qualified teaching staff, the pool out there at present is alarmingly small and I should think that anyone determined to establish themselves in this field would do well to bear in mind the parameters outlined above.

Using acting in remedial therapy

Acting has been used as a tool in various forms of treatment in psychiatry and psychology for a number of years, and some fascinating exploratory work in these areas is currently underway in universities and teaching hospitals. This is a highly specialist field and a richly rewarding one for those who feel attracted to acting as an activity, but who are interested in having a more direct effect on the welfare of others beyond simply getting up to perform in public.

Clearly, there are two ways of becoming involved in this work: either you become a medical and/or psychiatric practitioner, achieving first the appropriate qualifications, adding a knowledge of acting as part of the process, or you achieve a knowledge of the processes of acting and seek to use this as a drama specialist exploring therapy in collaboration with medical/psychiatric practitioners.

Listed at the end of this chapter is suggested general reading in this field, and some providers of courses which will open the way to a number of fascinating career options are listed at the back of this book.

Acting in the corporate world

Role-play has long been seen as a training accessory in preparing managers, sales executives, receptionists and many other employees in the business and commercial fields. Interestingly, some of this has come as a result of executives having previously experienced some form of drama-based training in the military. In order to 'psych-up' soldiers to be effective in battle, army commanders have for generations created pretend conflict situations. Interestingly, many of the training courses using aspects of acting now available to the business world have titles like 'Samurai', aimed at developing a killer instinct in business dealings.

Role-play is useful in almost any form of training and aspects of an actor's craft can be used – for example, Stanislavsky-style questions: What do I want? What effect do I want to make on the person I'm dealing with? – to achieve satisfactory outcomes in business transactions.

There are also, of course, technical communication skills, such as clear and effective vocal technique, appropriate and confident physical posture, which are part of an actor's stock in trade and which may become essential elements in effective business presentation.

The business world is fast waking up to the usefulness of this kind of training and many theatre practitioners are beginning to accrue useful supplementary income as a result. One eminent British theatre school, in fact, eventually dropped its corporate training programme, as the demand was so great that the school was in danger of becoming a training centre for businessmen rather than actors!

However, as with the training of actors, it's not necessarily the best actors who make the best teachers. Also, it's not necessarily the best trainers of actors who can teach business executives successfully. As with all teaching, you the trainer have to be clear as to the needs of your students – and a senior manager wishing to increase his sales in industrial adhesives has a quite different agenda from a 17-year-old beauty with her heart set on playing Ophelia at Stratford. He will also be used to recognizing value for money and is likely to be quick to decide whether or not you are providing her/him with an effective product.

Corporate training is a tough and increasingly competitive field. My advice to anyone contemplating entering it is to study the market carefully and to learn as much as you can about contemporary business practice. Learn the mind-set of high achievers, and of would-be high achievers, in the business world, and choose which of your acting-related skills you can offer effectively.

This is an area where any experience you may have already in the real world is as valuable as any skills you have accumulated as an actor. If you are either still working in business, or have contacts who are, it will be well worth asking to take part in training workshops, to observe and note how business and theatre skills may overlap.

The route into employment in this field is, as in so many other fields of work, often simply through personal contacts. However, management training consultancies are now beginning to take people with theatre-related skills on to their books. Once you are clear in your mind what specifically you have to offer the business world – be it voice teaching, role-playing workshops, or any other skill you may feel is marketable – I would suggest setting out your ideas in a concise proposal document and mailing it to a selection of management training companies in the major city nearest to where you live.

Suggested further reading

New Perspectives on Classroom Drama by G. Bolton (Simon & Schuster, London, 1992)

Dorothy Heathcote: Collected Writings on Education & Drama edited by Johnson & O'Neill (Hutchinson, London, 1984)

Dramatherapy – Theory and Practice for Teachers and Clinicians by S. Jennings (Croom Helm, UK, 1979)

Also: *International Guide* listed on page 64.

Disability, Theatre and Education by Richard Tomlinson (Souvenir, 1982)

Drama, Education and Special Needs, ed. Andy Kempe (Stanley Thornes, 1996)

9 | ACTING FOR A LIVING – ARE YOU REALLY SURE?

We've mentioned professional acting quite a lot so far and my guess is that a fair proportion of you who picked up this book did so because you have at least a vague feeling you might like to join The Profession, as older actors still rather grandly call it.

Let's deal with the cliché first – no, of course it isn't just a job, it is a calling, a vocation. One of Britain's most admired actors, Michael Bryant, has a classic response to people who ask whether they should try to become professional actors. 'If you want to be an actor – don't. If you're going to be an actor, you will.'

The problem with a calling, or a vocation, is that the dedication required of those affected by it carries a curse. You will need to eat, sleep and breathe acting if you are to fulfil your calling. And the more you train, the more you prepare your body and soul for performance, the more vital it becomes for you to practise your craft, to exercise your skills, to communicate to audiences through the expression of emotion, through the speaking of potent language. The curse, of course, comes into effect when suddenly you're Out of Work. Not 'resting', please, Out of Work. The neatest illustrations of the twilight world of the unemployed actor in Britain are currently the 'Hamlet' cartoons in *The Stage* newspaper, in which Hamlet, a rather forlorn pig, spends much of his time musing about the injustices of the world over a half-empty beer glass in his local bar.

If you've a nagging feeling that you won't feel complete until you've tried, if you torture yourself each time you see an actor playing a part so much less tellingly that you **know** you would have played it, then yes, probably you owe it to yourself really to explore the terrain thoroughly. But you must be clear-eyed. I could name you numbers of 50-plus-year-old actors who acknowledged years ago their sense of vocation, who trained properly, who have experienced heady periods of fame, of comparative riches (many you would recognize from television and film performances)

Cartoon © Harry Venning
Published in *The Stage* Newspaper Ltd, London

but who now have real problems between jobs in paying the rent, who have never been able to commit to a pension and may well be living in rented bed-sits because their fluctuating earning pattern has meant they were never able to raise a mortgage.

As they say in Yorkshire, think on. I doubt if there's a professional actor alive who at some point hasn't been told she or he has 'star potential'. Disappointment is corrosive, and leads to bitterness. On the other hand, it's my experience that actors are often the kindest, most generous, most realistic people you can ever hope to meet. And, often, they are wise: a wisdom that comes of years of detailed study of human behaviour. Once you've explored a human being, be they imaginary or real, and spent time living their life for an audience, then you've inevitably expanded your knowledge of *yourself*. A life of 'flying by the seat of your pants', of experiencing both rich fulfilment and bitter disappointment, means you have to develop a strong personal philosophy to help you cope.

This philosophy may include a determination to have more than one string to your bow and to make sure you always have an alternative source of income. Chapter 11 makes some suggestions in this regard. On the other hand, many actors see themselves purely as committed artists and prefer to suffer poverty rather than compromise their professional identity. Any way you slice it, the percentage of people who call themselves actors, who pay their dues to Equity and who actually make a decent living out of acting alone is very small.

Part of this is, of course, a question of pride: will your sense of dignity cope with being asked for your autograph at a bus-stop when you're not sure the cash in your pocket will cover the fare home? Can you rise above being asked 'Now then, have you done much acting at all, er, Elliot, sorry, er, Ellis' by a beardless television commercial director when you're 25 years into what you thought was quite a successful career? Can you handle being grilled by 17-year-old clerks as to whether you have any right to claim the unemployment benefit you so desperately need to collect before you can buy the family's weekly groceries?

If you've thought long and hard about all this and still have that nagging feeling that you really need to find out more, then I suggest you try taking a short 'introductory' professional training course. Some drama schools now offer 'access' courses, meant to provide preparation for auditioning for full-time training. Many summer courses are available: as I noted in Chapter 1, the starting point for this book was the range of questions asked by students on the RADA four-week Summer School, which offers an intensive 'taste' of drama-school training.

Examples of the summer school experience cutting both ways spring to mind. In one case, a regional careers officer came to RADA on a Careers Open Day and happened to confide in me that she'd always had, guess what, a sneaking suspicion that she ought to have been an actress . . . I suggested she take a place on the summer school, and she did. At the end of her four weeks at RADA, she came to my office grinning broadly, saying she'd had the time of her life, had loved every minute, and was now convinced the last thing she'd ever want to do was risk being a professional actor. From now on she would use all the stuff she'd learned on the summer school to beef up her hobby, as an active member of her local amateur theatre company. In another case, a young man from a theatrical family came to the summer school, to test whether he really wanted to train, or whether he was being influenced by his background. He found the degree of training available on the summer school just enough to stimulate a real appetite for more, auditioned successfully for the three-year programme, and at the time of going to press is embarking on what looks to be a very promising career.

When I was at school and experiencing the first twitches of the acting bug, I looked in the school library at a book not unlike this one, offering quotes from famous actors and actresses as advice for 1950s wannabees. Laurence Olivier's advice was neat: look at a copy of *The Spotlight* and see how many photographs you recognize . . . It's even more telling advice today. *The Spotlight* is the professional directory of British actors and carries photos of virtually every single British person offering her/himself for employment. In the 1950s there were a few hundred pages – now there are eight volumes, and literally thousands of entries . . . A glance at the *Back Stage* newspaper in America opens a door to the teeming New York acting scene, with thousands of actors seeking recognition, or just attention, striving in an unforgiving world just to be noticed.

Anyway, if you still want to find out more, check out the list of access training and summer school contacts, and then go on to read the remaining chapters.

10 | TRAINING FOR ACTING

Before we embark on reviewing the options for professional training, it's worth asking a few questions.

To start with, is a formal training necessary for everyone who wants to be an actor? The answer is clearly, no, not for everyone. There are major stars who've never been near a drama school: Bob Hoskins, for instance, landed his first acting job when he went along to keep an actor pal company at an audition and ended up by being offered a part himself. Is it enough simply to follow an academic education, and 'train' through playing big parts in the university dramsoc? Again, for some people it clearly is – look at Emma Thompson. Are university Drama degrees the equivalent of drama school diplomas? The answer to that depends to some extent on where you live – professional training courses are available in many universities, and some famous acting schools are faculties within universities, especially in North America. However, the pattern of training options in the United Kingdom can be confusing, as many of the hitherto independent drama schools have now formed associations with universities so that they can offer degree qualifications. I will attempt to clarify the situation later in this chapter.

Most people with serious professional aspirations seem to consider a period of formal training essential and the majority of actors pursuing successful careers have undergone training of some sort. Is it still possible to train through an 'apprenticeship' of gaining work experience in amateur and repertory companies? This is far less possible than it was, say, 20 years ago. Very few regional repertory theatres produce plays all the year round and fewer still support any sort of 'permanent' company, with actors on long-term contracts. In America, the distinction between amateur and professional in some regional theatres is less marked than in the United Kingdom, and thus acting experience may be gained while still maintaining a 'day job'.

It is true that some major producing companies, such as the Royal Shakespeare Company and the Royal National Theatre in London provide in-house training for actors – usually related to the specific needs of particular productions – but the majority of new, unknown actors recruited by these companies tend still to have first undertaken a formal training elsewhere.

We've already discussed the difference in attitude between amateur and professional approaches to acting: I think you'll find that most high-quality amateur companies would recommend undertaking a training course before stepping out into the professional world.

But most acting schools seem to have theatre-based curricula – if all you want is to be a television or movie star, why would you want to train for the theatre? The answer is that you might be lucky and 'make it' in front of a camera without a theatre training – but you're then in hock to the vagaries of television and film economics. If you've made a television series and become famous, you might be offered other parts, but then again you might not – television history is littered with the husks of careers of once-famous soap stars. And without the training, as we've commented elsewhere, it's darned difficult then to expand your work opportunities to include appearing in theatres seating a thousand or more punters, if your vocal delivery is geared only to providing dialogue for a microphone a few inches above your head.

It's worth mentioning that the pace of creating training opportunities for people with disabilities is beginning to speed up, after many years of neglect. Pioneering work has been undertaken by professional producing companies like GRAEAE and Candoco; courses and facilities are being developed in a number of training establishments, as awareness grows of the need to provide equal chances of expressing creativity for everyone. In the lists at the end of this book are contact organizations which will have relevant information.

Which school?

So, assuming you decide to seek a training, given the huge range of drama schools advertised in the relevant publications, how can you tell which are the good ones? Well, you have to research the field. Just because a drama school publishes large and attractive advertising copy doesn't mean it's a brilliant school. Enquire as to its track-record – in particular its recent track-record – in producing successful actors. If possible, talk to actors who have experience of courses at the schools in which you are interested: as indicated elsewhere in this book, not all courses are necessarily appropriate to all actors.

As I pointed out in the introduction, this book doesn't seek to supply all possible information about acting on a worldwide basis. There are, of course, major training centres for actors in Europe (we have already mentioned the LeCoq school in Paris) and there is a trickle of European mainland students beginning to appear in British schools. The fact is, however, that most training is aimed at finding effective ways of expressing texts and, therefore, complete command of the language is a prerequisite.

Let us look briefly at the options facing would-be actors in the major concentrations of English speakers, in North America, Australia, New Zealand and the United Kingdom.

United States and Canada

Clearly, North America has huge and diverse acting traditions. In Canada, there are still strong cultural links with Europe, and in Montreal the National Theatre School has both Anglophone and Francophone faculties. At the present time Canada seems to be experiencing a boom in new writing for the theatre and there is a lot of activity in fringe and mainstream theatre, corresponding with some dynamic creativity in film and television.

In the United States, while the theatre has produced many superb playwrights – O'Neil, Williams, Miller, Mamet – the two great traditions which have had a direct influence on the development of acting seem to me to have been the Musical and the Cinema. The American popular singing traditions, alongside those of marching bands, cheer-leader troupes, etc., have claimed the stage musical as a prime area of American expertise, Andrew Lloyd Webber notwithstanding. Meanwhile, the small acting studio, developed from the American version of the Stanislavsky tradition, has produced for the cinema emotional acting of remarkable detail and intensity.

The enormous size of these countries also makes for significant differences from the scene in the United Kingdom. Regional theatres often have status (and budgets) comparable to 'national' theatres in smaller countries, but in North America particularly, are often part of a university campus and serve as a venue for a wide range of productions – amateur (or 'community') theatre, professional touring shows, semi-professional productions, often with a professional director and a mixture of paid and unpaid performers.

There are several routes for potential actors in North America: via the regional university drama department, via the (comparatively few) conservatoire performing arts colleges, and via the small studio acting schools, usually found in the major cities.

The latter have developed in the wake of the Stanislavsky-inspired movement mentioned earlier and offer very concentrated training – often part-time, often over long periods. They reflect a different pattern of working culture, wherein the actor will automatically return to his 'acting studio' throughout his career, something I think British actors would do well to emulate.

Similarly, the distinction between 'straight' and 'musical' actors is much more blurred in America than in the United Kingdom, and many performers attend regular dance and singing classes as well as acting sessions.

Interestingly, in New York, a number of the famous actors' studio schools (such as the Stella Adler and the Lee Strasberg Actors' Studio) are now associated with the New York University Tisch School of Performing Arts and it is possible to include modules of studio-training in a more comprehensive degree programme.

University degrees in North America have a different agenda from the traditional British academic degree and are often much more geared to vocational training. A regional university in North America may well have performance facilities to make any British university drama tutor green with envy. At SUNY Purchase University in New York State, for instance, there are two theatre spaces to rival those at the Royal National Theatre in London.

Many of the well-known conservatoire-style schools, such as those at Yale and Juilliard are still concerned with awarding degrees, but have an agenda for teaching performance skills more related to training for professional-level performance than most university drama departments in the United Kingdom. In New York, there are two smaller, dedicated schools with their roots in that city's home-grown theatrical traditions: the Circle in the Square, which began life in Greenwich Village and now lives just off Times Square, and the Neighbourhood Playhouse in mid-town, which has a wonderful library and an atmosphere not a million miles away from that which pervaded RADA in the days before its multi-million pound refurbishment: well-used, like a much-loved storybook.

The comparative scarcity of conservatoire schools in the United States and Canada has meant in recent years that many American actors have chosen to supplement their training by going to Britain to take short courses in the drama schools there. At RADA, we now have several courses which are specifically geared to providing Shakespearian training for professional or graduate actors and several other schools do the same. The student intake for these courses is often largely from North America and sometimes there are courses which are organized in collaboration between American and European colleges – for example, NYU Tisch and RADA, or Austin State University Texas and Rose Bruford College, London.

Again, partly because of the vast distances involved, partly because they tend to be much more hard-headed in terms of the importance of earning money, many actors in the United States settle for working on a part-time basis, following parallel careers as real-estate managers or whatever, and keep up their acting by performing in either fringe shows in the cities rehearsed during their spare time, or take part in semi-professional productions – often at the regional university theatres mentioned above. Not to say that fully professional regional repertory theatre doesn't exist in North America – fine examples exist, for example at Philadelphia, Stratford Ontario, Pasadena, etc.

My own perception is that, if you're an American or Canadian actor with an inclination to concentrate on musical theatre, you are probably best off seeking training in the United States, although some schools in the United Kingdom are beginning to offer musical theatre courses alongside their more traditional British-style training (one such is the Guildford School of Acting.)

If you live in America and want a general training as an actor, then there are many good courses available, and the directory listed at the back of this book gives much more information than there is space for here. If at any time you feel a need to take advantage of the more classical training available in Britain, then I offer a small selection from the wide range available. There is also a full list of the British Conference of Drama Schools on pages 143–5.

Australia and New Zealand

The acting training scene in these countries seems to be not dissimilar to that of the United States, with a range of performing arts faculties in universities and a relatively small number of dedicated conservatories. Not surprisingly, given the size of the country, training is organized on a regional basis. However, there is a national Arts umbrella in the shape of the Australia Council (address at the end of this book) which will be able to supply information about the whole Australian theatre scene.

As well as acting and theatre arts courses, technical theatre courses are available – for example at the Victorian College in Melbourne, and some specialist courses for musical theatre performers, as at the National Academy of Singing and Dramatic Art in Christchurch, New Zealand.

The colleges nearest in style to British drama schools are NIDA in Sydney, the Victorian College in Melbourne, the drama course at Flinders University, the Western Australia Academy of Performing Arts and the National Academy in New Zealand.

In both Australia and New Zealand, incidentally, there are thriving traditions of youth and children's theatre and you will find some suggested contacts at the end of this book.

An invaluable guide to training in this part of the world is *Directions*, published annually by *Lowdown* Magazine in North Adelaide.

Training in the United Kingdom

There is in existence in Britain an alliance of quality control organizations which creates a benchmark of excellence. These are respectively the Conference of Drama Schools, which is the 'umbrella' association of 'craft-based' training schools and the National Council for Drama Training, which is the organization recognized by the performance industries as accrediting the courses on offer; this accreditation has also been used as a benchmark by local authorities in deciding whether or not to award grants. All the schools in the CDS have to be investigated by an NCDT accreditation team every three to five years in order to maintain the status of their courses. The NCDT visiting panels include experts in the field of drama training and practitioners from the trade itself, including employers and the relevant trade unions. (Equity, for instance, now automatically grants membership to students graduating from NCDT-accredited full-length, full-time vocational training courses.)

The fact is that you have a better chance of receiving a decent training on an accredited course than elsewhere. Not to say that good training doesn't happen outside of the CDS and NCDT, but theirs is, at the time of writing, the only nationally recognized 'yardstick'. There is, as already noted, a huge range of schools offering training outside of the CDS, and many universities now offer degress in drama, some of which are advertised as providing professional acting training. (To confuse matters even further, many of the CDS schools now offer 'degrees in acting', the degrees being validated by an associated university. We'll come back to this shortly.)

But, for now, let's assume you decide to apply to a CDS School. How do you tell which is the most appropriate for you? There are, at the time of going to press, some 19 schools in the Conference. Well, to start with, the CDS now helpfully publishes a handbook summarizing the prospectae of all the schools and there is now a CDS Website available on the Internet supplying the same information. (Addresses for both listed at the end of this book.)

Beyond that, you have to make enquiries, both of the schools themselves and along the grapevine. Try to find out which recently trained actors you admire went to which school – the quality of training in every school will differ according to the calibre of its Principal and staff. We at RADA, for instance, while immensely proud of the fact that Sir John Gielgud trained at our school can hardly claim credit for a graduate of the class of 1925! (We do, however, claim credit for the most recent RSC Juliet, the new star of the *Hornblower* film series, the present artistic director of the Globe Theatre, leading actors in recent Shakespeare productions by the Royal National Theatre, Cheek by Jowl, etc.)

There may well be aspects of the craft for which you have a particular inclination. We discussed, for instance, mime as a useful skill if you want to work in children's theatre. As it happens, at the time of writing the movement department at the Royal Scottish Academy has teachers who trained at the Le Coq school in Paris, which includes a strong mime element in its training. (Not that the RSAMD offers training just for mime-based children's theatre actors – theirs is a full and distinguished curriculum!) If, on the other hand, you feel you have special gifts in the field of musical theatre, the Guildford School of Acting has developed a highly successful course emphasizing this aspect of training. In the field of 'classical' work, many other schools have long histories of providing actors for the RSC, the National and other major companies – Central,

RADA, Drama Centre, the Guildhall, LAMDA, RSAMD, Bristol Old Vic, Webber-Douglas, Rose Bruford, etc. – but then their graduates also appear in television 'soaps', West End musicals, television and radio commercials – all the places where professional actors earn a crust.

In making your enquiries, you may find that the teaching style of one school appeals to you more than any other. Drama Centre, for example, has produced some superbly trained actors through its own version of Stanislavsky-based teaching, with a specific agenda of rigorously disciplined exercises and rehearsal techniques. At other schools, the curriculum may be more eclectic, drawing on a different range of influences – the difference is in approach.

A word of warning: check the size of the intake at any school you are considering. Most of the really good schools take around 30 students per year on to each main acting course. This allows for sensible class sizes – no class group at RADA, for example, is bigger than 17, usually subdivided to allow teaching in much smaller groups, where necessary down to a one-to-one situation. It also shows a realistic attitude to the needs of the performance industries and the size of the job-market. But the demand for places is high, and students' fees are the main source of income for many schools which are private institutions, not in receipt of public subsidy. So the temptation is to take on more and more students, with a corresponding drop in the amount of quality teaching.

Whichever way you choose to be trained, your career chances, in terms of exposure, are higher at the CDS schools. The fact is that most major casting directors and agents attend the final-year 'showcase' productions at CDS schools, as it's in their interest to do so, given that so many of the biggest earning current stars were first 'spotted' at drama school. By the way, if you like the idea of training in one of the several excellent out-of-London schools, such as Bristol Old Vic, the Welsh College of Music and Drama, or the Royal Scottish, bear in mind that these colleges all ensure exposure to London-based as well as regionally based employers. Each of these schools brings the final-year students to a well-advertised 'showcase' at a central London venue; and the Royal Scottish at least offers travel subsidy to any London-based potential employers who wish to visit productions at the Academy's theatres in Glasgow.

There is a strong argument for regional training, especially if you feel you would rather be based in an area other than London. In the current climate of decentralization in the UK, the regions are developing substantial cultural and entertainment industries, with a concomitant demand for local, and locally trained, talent. Scotland, especially, has in many ways a healthier theatrical scene than England with, for example, more producing professional theatres per capita and a smaller population of actors.

On other schools, universities and finding funds

But what of the options outside of the CDS 'stable' of drama schools? Again, research at the time of applying is essential. There are schools outside the CDS who have trained successfully a number of serious actors, but you should enquire carefully as to any school's overall track-record, its class sizes, the credentials of the teachers and whether any claims to artistic excellence are matched by a realistic approach to the demands of the profession.

What of the 'university option'? Is doing a course at university a realistic alternative to going to drama school? Perhaps the most eloquent comment on this is in a plain statistic; at present approximately a third of the students on the 3-year diploma in acting course at RADA already hold university degrees. The fact is that universities are institutes of higher education. The very specific requirements of skills training for the performing arts demand more concentrated schedules than are available to a student whose timetable needs to include substantial space for academic research, essay writing, in-depth reading, etc. A degree in drama from a good university is a wonderfully enriching asset for anyone interested in the performing arts – it is simply not the same thing as an intensive, specific training.

So why do some drama schools offer 'degrees in acting'? The answer to this is crudely economic and political. Historically, most students accepting offers of places on university courses have been eligible for 'mandatory' local authority grants, i.e. grants which would automatically be awarded. Candidates for training diploma courses (and this included most professional training courses in drama and dance) were allowed to apply only for 'discretionary' grants – i.e. the local authority had the option to turn down any such requests for funding. In this context, the status of a course would often be taken into account, in terms of accreditation by a recognized authority such as the NCDT.

Reorganisation of the higher and further education systems in the late 1980s and early 1990s meant that places on degree courses increased hugely as many of the old polytechnics were turned into universities. The crunch was that, as more and more people applied for mandatory grants for degree courses at the new universities, and as local government spending became more and more restricted by central government, the budgets for 'discretionary' funding dwindled and in many cases dried up altogether.

The response of some of the CDS schools was to enter into arrangements with universities, whereby their training diplomas in acting were 'upgraded' to degrees, and a certain academic content was introduced into the curriculum to allow the associated university to validate the degree, thus permitting undergraduates in the acting degree courses to qualify for mandatory grants.

Other schools, including RADA, chose not to take that route, on the grounds indicated above – i.e., that university education and craft training were two different things, both deserving equal, but separate, funding policies. At the time of writing this political and philosophical debate continues; the short-term effect has been that students choosing to take a diploma in acting as opposed to a degree have had a tough time of it these last few years, often having to work their way through college by waiting tables or working in bars at night and at weekends; many students have accrued substantial debts.

In terms of the quality of the training for actors, I believe that in many of the degree-awarding CDS schools the new academic content has been quite limited, and that where high practical training standards were applied before, high standards have been maintained – the same tutors are employed to teach the same skills and the end results are not dissimilar to those of the old diplomas. However, nobody pretends that a casting director will cast Hamlet because he's got a 2:1 for a dissertation on the Use of the Tongue-tip in post-Renaissance English Pronunciation ….

By the time this book is published, it is quite likely that the whole picture regarding funding for dance and drama training will have changed, as the new government is currently reviewing the situation, and there are rumours of substantial changes afoot. At the time of writing, the only advice we can offer with regard to funding your training is for you to question your local authority closely as to the availability or non-availability of grants, watch the national press for political developments and be prepared, if necessary, to become your own fund-raiser.

At RADA, once we have decided to offer a place on either the core acting diploma course or core stage-management course we will work with the student concerned to develop a funding strategy; the Registrar and the

Technical Courses Administrator spend weeks and months hounding local authorities, charitable trust funds and benevolent wealthy individuals for financial support for individual students. With any luck, these efforts will become redundant; in the meantime, if we think you're good enough to train, we'll give you as much support as we can muster.

What can I expect from training?

To give some idea of the density of the training now available at a CDS school, I list at the end of this chapter some of the topics you may expect to be covered by classes during the first two years at a British drama school. (Obviously courses vary, and this list is by no means comprehensive, but it should give you some idea of the range of demands made on students' time and concentration.)

The three terms of the final year are spent effectively as a member of a repertory company, with each student acting in a range of plays (each production under the supervision of a professional director and designer) plus programmes of audition pieces presented to an invited audience of agents and casting directors. (These last are called at RADA the 'Tree' presentations, after the Academy's founder Sir Herbert Beerbohm Tree.)

You will see from the range of subjects being taught that there is not much spare time: the course seeks to provide a practical acquaintance with the acting demands of a wide range of writing styles backed-up with in-depth physical and vocal training. In other countries this kind of conservatoire training is spread over four years; at present it's difficult enough for students to find funds for three years, let alone four. So another element in the training is to try to encourage in actors an awareness of the need for ongoing training, to carry on the learning process throughout the career, in the way that professional musicians and dancers never cease to enhance their skills through 'taking class'.

Another element in the course is the interface with the world of professional acting. For the first two years, schools discourage exposure – for example at RADA we do not allow active students to appear in public shows until the end of term 6, at the very end of the second year. When you are going through a period of intense training your focus is on you and your equipment, and you need space to make mistakes out of the spotlight. However, in the final year, acting students are directed by professional directors in showcase productions which are also designed by professional designers who work with the stage-management and technical students. Throughout the year, as well as appearing in shows the audience for which will invariably have a high content of represntatives from the performance industries seeking new talent, we also run a professional advice service, retaining a careers consultant who supplies advice in regard to dealing with agents, preparing your CV, what to do about income tax, Equity, etc. Most of the CDS schools have their own version of this.

A question constantly asked is – What about one-year courses? Many people feel, especially if they've completed a drama degree at a university, that they can't cope with a further three years as a student. Surely you can learn enough in one year to give you the technical knowledge you need to support a career in acting?

Again, for some people this may be true, but many others recognize that the depth of training available on a conservatoire course is unique and has to take time – I've already quoted the number of university graduates currently at RADA. But some fine schools offer one- or two-year, post-graduate courses and, if you really feel this is the route for you, then you should check out the courses on offer, in the way recommended above for the three-year options.

You need to think hard about what your priorities are. When I welcome the new first-year acting students to RADA each year I always tell them 'You are going to change – whether you like it or not, you are going to change.' You may think that just to learn to improve your speaking and moving is a comparatively simple matter. Maybe it is, and maybe you can learn all you need to learn by taking a shorter, simpler course.

All I can tell you is that when I was 21 I was too impatient to go back to college after I'd finished my degree. There was a lot of work to be had out there in the repertory theatres, and in television, so I attained a sort of apprenticeship out in the field. It's much more difficult to do that now, as I've already noted, and, after six years of watching young actors develop at a high-grade drama school, I honestly regret missing out on the experience. The cliché that if a thing's worth doing it's worth doing properly holds very true. If you're going to be a professional musician, you have to get to know your instrument down to its last molecule, to make it do exactly what you want it to, so that you can move, exhilarate and delight your audience at will. If you're going to be an actor, **you** are your instrument.

How do I get in to a school?

So, you've reviewed the options in terms of the courses available, you've started to address the question of finding finance, now how are you going to set about gaining a place on the course of your choice?

Do you need to have any previously gained qualifications?

For most acting diploma courses the only criteria are demonstrably trainable acting talent and a good working knowledge of the English language. Degree courses may require formal academic qualifications, such as 'A' levels.

Any course worth its salt will require you to audition. Some schools have a more exhaustive audition process than others. At RADA your application (with which you will have included a registration fee, as with all the CDS schools) earns you the right to a preliminary audition. RADA draws on the services of a professional audition panel, made up of distinguished actors, directors and teachers. Your initial presentation will be before two members of the panel. We will ask you to have prepared two monologues, of no more than three minutes each, one classical piece and one modern. If your audition goes well, you may be invited to a 're-call' audition, usually a week or two later. At this you will meet several further members of the panel, plus the Academy's Principal and the Head of the Acting Course. You will be asked to re-present your two pieces and also to sing a song, unaccompanied. (This isn't a singing test, more an indication as to your 'ear' and your sense of your own vocal range.) You will then be invited to chat with the panel and tell them about your reasons for applying to drama school. If you succeed at this audition, you will be invited to the Academy for a whole day's 'audition workshop', when you will be observed taking part in various classes, along with 15 or so other candidates, and finally present a new monologue at the end of the day.

You may then have to wait quite a long time before we make up our minds: sometimes we offer straight away, but more usually we wait to build up a picture of the sort of class group we might put together from the range of people making it through to this particular year's shortlist. The entire audition process runs from November through until the end of May, and along the way includes preliminary audition sessions in Manchester, Newcastle, Birmingham and New York. (Other schools also audition in other parts of the English-speaking world.) While RADA tends to receive more audition applications than most other British schools (currently about 1,400 for the 16 male and 16 female places) the process is similar with most CDS academies.

Is age a factor?

Few schools offering a three-year professional training accept students below the age of 17 – however, there are now some excellent foundation courses intended for teenage students available in colleges specializing in the performing arts, such as the BRIT School – see the list at the end of this book. Theoretically, most schools have no upper age limit, but experience has shown that people beyond their thirties often have difficulty in taking on board the personal re-organization required by this type of training. But far be it from me to discourage anyone who has a burning sense of vocation, at any stage in their life. A number of celebrated actors came late into the profession: as I've said elsewhere, if you have reached a certain age and the desire to act still gnaws, then it may well be a good idea to test the water in one of the shorter courses on offer before pitching for a place on a full-time three-year course.

How important is the choice of audition material?

Bear in mind that you may be scheduled at the end of a long, full day, and if you're the fifteenth Juliet the panel have seen since 9 o'clock you're going to have to be pretty damned good. Having said that, if someone comes on and gives a really fresh, revealing 'spin' to a familiar text, then attention will be paid. It's worth looking out for unusual texts, providing you know you can use them to show yourself to be alert, resourceful and sensitive. As a general rule, it's not too good an idea to choose a piece a long way away from your own age: there is a danger that, in trying to create for instance, an impression of an elderly person, you will clutter the truth of your interpretation with unnecessary 'old' acting – squashing your voice, or creating seemingly arthritic movements.

Don't try to be too clever – ask yourself a few simple questions when you're learning the text. What are this character's exact circumstances? Given these circumstances, what are the key words the character uses in each sentence? How might these circumstances inform the way these key words are said, and how does this affect the sense and the impact of the whole piece?

Different schools have different policies with regard to audition texts. Some schools prescribe certain standard pieces; at RADA we go the other way and send candidates a list of pieces we'd rather they didn't do, either because we're bored to tears with them or because we don't think they give an actor a fair chance of showing his or her ability.

Try to build up a range of pieces, so that you have repertoire to offer the panel, should they ask to see you do something demonstrating, say, your comic side if they feel your initial choice is too serious.

It's not usually a good idea to 'cobble together' monologues made up of lines from dialogue; if a good playwright needs to develop a situation with a soliloquy or monologue, then she or he will write one. Lines filleted from a conversation and then stitched together always sound odd, and you really are not helping yourself as a performer by not choosing a speech which has been carefully constructed by an expert author.

Sometimes students offer self-written speeches. Again, far be it from me to discourage creativity, but my advice would be that, even if you have a piece of your own which you (and more importantly others whose opinion you respect) firmly believe is a good and appropriate showpiece, it should be kept in reserve and offered as an alternative should the audition panel ask to see something in addition to your initial presentation of an established text.

If you feel that your piece requires you to 'include' the audition panel – for example, if the character is addressing the audience directly – it's usually a good idea to pitch your eyeline just above and beyond where the auditioners are sitting, as though to an invisible 'second row'. To have an actor fixing your gaze eyeball to eyeball is often embarrassing and often very distracting.

How many schools should I apply to?

Don't put your all your eggs in one basket. My heart sinks when we ask a candidate which other schools they're applying for and they say 'Oh, I'm only applying to RADA'. For a start, as I've outlined above, there are other excellent schools offering comparable training and, given the mathematical odds against getting in any of the good schools, it makes absolute sense to hedge your bets. There are, obviously, some sensationally good actors who either didn't get into RADA because they didn't fit the group picture the Principal was trying to build that year, or because the audition panel simply missed a trick – they're only human. There are also some stars who didn't apply to RADA because they preferred to train elsewhere.

Do your research, decide which schools make sense for you and then save up the money you need to pay the audition registration fees.

Remember the dictum '. . . if you're going to be an actor, you will'. You may well fail to get a place at one of your chosen schools the first time around. Providing you've really got the fire in your belly, providing your passion is there and you maintain a realistic eye on your own need to improve and develop, you may well get in next year. At RADA we've taken candidates at the second and third attempt. The important thing is to keep monitoring yourself – it may be that your enthusiasm is misplaced and that, after several failed auditions, the penny will drop that acting isn't, in fact, what you're cut out to do for the rest of your life. Nothing wrong with that – that's a bit of self-knowledge that will stand you in good stead in whatever else you decide to do. Never forget that in turning away from acting as a career, you may well be saving yourself years of heartache and bitter disappointment. You may also find that having trained as an actor, extremely satisfying and even lucrative career paths open up in other related fields a few years down the track. The wonderful thing about developing yourself as an actor is that you inevitably develop yourself as a person at the same time, with infinite horizons and endless possibilities.

Some of the topics you can expect to be covered in a drama school training

- **Voice**.
- **Speech**.
- **Phonetics**.
- **Dialect**.
- **Text analysis: verse structure**, etc., in Shakespeare and other classical writers.
- **Text analysis: modern texts**.
- **Sight reading**.
- **Modern script structure**, including at some schools, courses in playwriting and/or devising.
- **Movement** – various disciplines, depending on the school – e.g. some may relate to the Alexander Technique, and/or the

work of Rudolph Laban, or of Litz Pisk, etc. Many movement courses include an element of studying animal behaviour.

■ Some schools have a strong **Mime** element in their training, others place less emphasis on this.

■ **Physical skills**, such as Tumbling.

■ **Combat** for the stage, both armed and unarmed.

■ **Period dance**.

■ **Modern dance** for the stage.

■ **Period 'style'** as expressed through movement and text, and awareness of different styles of staging – proscenium in the round, arena, etc.

■ **Singing** – solo and choral.

■ **Music rudiments**, including, at some schools, learning an instrument.

■ **Acting exercises**, derived from the work of Stanislavsky.

■ **Rehearsing** for presentations of various periods and styles of text – Shakespeare, Jacobean, Restoration, nineteenth century and modern 'realist' writers, modern American writing, etc.

■ **Acting for cameras and microphones**.

11 | THE BUSINESS OF ACTING

Let us now assume that you've completed your formal training and are now on offer to the world as a professional actor. How will you set about finding work? Let's be realistic – while you're looking for acting work, you may well need to do other jobs just to survive, so I've included some suggestions for sheer survival in Chapter 12. For now, let's address some vital questions about building a career as an actor.

Is there an 'essential handbook'?

You mean, other than this one? Yes there is, or rather, yes there are several, published in the various English-speaking parts of the world. The indispensable British publication is called *Contacts*. It's published by *The Spotlight* (of which more later) in October of every year and is an essential directory of contact numbers and addresses for virtually all the people and organizations you'll need to know about: agents, casting directors, film, television and theatre production companies. London and regional theatres, professional organizations, touring 'digs', photographers, etc. It costs only a few pounds and is worth every penny. Call *The Spotlight* to check the current price (see listing at the end of this book).

More specifically geared to actors, and with more detailed information, is *The Actor's Handbook*, again listed at the end of this book.

In America, the equivalent of *Contacts* is *The Back Stage Handbook for Performing Artists*, and in Australia, you need *Stage Whispers*. (See listings at the end of the book for how to obtain them.)

Do I need an agent, and if so how do I get one?

If you've just left drama school, you'll know that most of the talk amongst your fellow students during the final year has been about Finding an Agent. You may have already formed a relationship with one. The question usually asked is 'Have you "signed" with an agent?' This can be rather misleading, as by no means all agents expect actors to sign contracts binding them to a business relationship. Some do, but more often (in London, at any rate) business is conducted on a 'gentlemen's agreement' basis – i.e., the agent agrees verbally to represent the actor in all matters of acting employment and the actor agrees in return to allow all contracts to be processed by the agent's office, and all money to be paid via the agent, at which point the agent deducts an agreed percentage. (Most professional contracts have a sub-clause for you to sign authorizing all payments to be sent to the agent.)

However, in these days of increasing legislation and litigation, it may seem to you to be sensible to sign a contract with an agent. If the agent produces an agreement for you to sign, have it checked by the Equity (or other relevant union, see address at the end of this book) legal department before you do.

Actors tend to work on a 'sole agent' basis – in other words you agree to let the one agency handle all your professional work. This is quite different from the world of freelance musicians, for instance, which is much more promiscuous – agents tend to be general 'fixers' who arrange to supply musicians to employers on a job-to-job basis, and any musician can approach any fixer for work at any time. The exception to the sole agent system in the world of acting is that sometimes an actor's 'main' agent will agree to the client getting specialist work through a separate specialist agent, the most usual example of this being voice-over work. There are certain agents who handle only voice work and try to arrange bookings for actors which fit in with their other commitments. (Another example might be in the case of an actor who is also a stunt performer, or a fight arranger.)

But we're getting ahead of ourselves; if you haven't got an agent, do you really need one? Well, I have known a number of successful actors who have survived splendidly without agents, but the fact is that the system tends to be agent-orientated, especially in film and television. Having said that, in the early stages of your career it's sometimes better to spend some time building up your own portfolio of contacts until such time as you find an agent who is right for you. If an agent has approached you after a show at drama school and seems keen to represent you, make as many enquiries as you can about her or his credentials.

Flick through the entries in *The Spotlight* directory (or the equivalent – e.g. the *Players' Guide* in the United States, *Showcast* in Australia) as to who else the agency represents. It may be that they have many clients, but none of whom you recognize – some of the less reputable agents have huge numbers of clients on their books, in the hope that at least some of them will be paying commission some of the time.

The Spotlight organization in London runs an agency advisory service for their subscribers: they make it their business to monitor the agent scene, and are able to advise you as to the suitability or otherwise of an agency you may consider approaching. You'll have to subscribe to *The Spotlight* (or its equivalent in your part of the world) anyway. *The Spotlight* is a five-volume directory, with photos of every actor in Britain – virtually all directors and casting directors refer to it, and it now has a fancy hi-tech 'laser cast' version which is used internationally. Scrape enough money together to pay for your entry – if you've been to a CDS school you will already probably be in their 'new actors' edition. Once you're a subscriber, you can call them and ask for an appointment to see one of their advisors.

What sort of commission will an agent demand?

Historically, agents took 10 per cent of all the money processed by their office. Sometimes nowadays it's 12.5 per cent, sometimes more. Agents charge varying rates: for example some may take only 10 per cent on regional theatre work, but 12.5 per cent on television and film contracts and as much as 15 per cent on television commercials. Whatever the deal they offer, again check it out with Equity and/or *Spotlight* before you agree.

What do I need to spend money on in order to get started?

Good question. If you're setting yourself up as a professional, you have to get into a business-like way of thinking. You are offering a service – you may see it as an artistic, cultural or even an educational or social service – but it's basically the same as setting yourself up as a window cleaner or hairdresser. You need equipment and you need advertising.

As with all freelance workers, much of what you invest in legitimate expenses is claimable against income tax. See under 'Accountancy'.

Here are some of the things you need to budget for:

■ An effective **means of being contacted**. At the very least you need a **telephone with answering service**, and many actors nowadays have also a pager and/or an e-mail address. You will find in the relevant trade papers advertisements for voice-mail and e-mail service companies, who will provide you with a low-cost 24-hour, 365-days-per-year permanent point of contact, so that even if you are travelling, or for some reason don't have a permanent base, you can always be contacted. Every casting director will work through a list of candidates when they're setting up auditions or interviews, and if they – or your agent – can't get hold of you, or at least leave a message on their first call, they'll move on to the next name and almost certainly won't bother to call you a second time.

■ Relevant skills. As we've already observed, your equipment is you, so you need to decide how much time you're going to spend on **professional coaching** – in voice, dance, singing, whatever – to keep your performance skills at the ready. A good idea is to join the Actors' Centre, or a dance/fitness studio, where you can join group classes, which are less expensive than individual tuition.

■ A basic **make-up kit, if you are going to work in the theatre**. In books of this sort, when I was starting out, there would be an exhaustive chapter on make-up technique, as it was considered an essential skill. In modern productions, even in 'classical theatre', make-up is less of an issue than it used to be, partly because of improved lighting, partly because it's simply become unfashionable, and in theatre shows is often dispensed with altogether. If a special effect is required, companies will sometimes hire in a make-up artist. In film and television, make-up artists are hired in as a matter of course, but in the theatre professional actors are still required to provide their own standard make-up if required.

All actors should have a basic knowledge of how to make their faces at least more visible in a large theatre, and most drama courses will provide you with a basic training. In terms of kit, I hope it's not sexist to note that many female actors will already possess at least some items of everyday 'street' make-up, which for most stage purposes are all that's required. For either sex, you basically need a light liquid foundation, a 'blusher' or other means of creating shading, an eyeliner, mascara and powder. If you want to get into dedicated stage make-up, Kryolan make a range of products available in most countries.

■ Clothing/costume: As well as **clothing for class**, and **for auditions likely to involve dance or movement** – thus **leotards**, **tights**, etc. – you will need to keep a reasonable range of outfits to allow you to present various aspects of your personality at interviews and auditions. In America, actors sometimes go to great pains to dress at auditions exactly for the part – even to the extent of hiring costumes. I don't necessarily support this idea, which can be disastrously self-defeating if your advance information is wrong – but it makes sense, for example, to turn up wearing a tie if you're hoping to play a bank manager, or something light and youthful if you're up for Juliet.

When I first joined Equity, there were clauses in the Esher Standard Contract for Repertory requiring male actors to supply if required 'one lounge suit and one evening suit', and actresses 'one casual outfit and one evening gown'. Mercifully this has long since been dropped, but many actors still keep an eye open for potentially useful bits of costume: if you've got something in your own wardrobe which is clearly much more appropriate to a particular character than anything the management can find, you may well be able to hire it to the company for use in the production. There are still a few actors who specialize in pantomime 'dame' and build up fantastic collections of comic (and often surreal) costumes, which they then hire out as a separate item 'in tandem' with themselves when negotiating contracts to perform in Christmas shows. (Non-Brits may not be sure what a panto dame is – please check out the glossary at the end of this book.)

■ **Union dues**. Although the power-base of trades unions has changed in most Western countries in recent years, and it is not always obligatory to be in a relevant union in order to be employable, to be involved in a professional association seems to me to be part of your working identity. In Britain, Equity is still recognized as the negotiating body for working conditions and basic rates of pay in virtually all areas of acting. In America, Equity applies mainly to theatre work, with acting employment issues in the media being covered by the Screen Actors' Guild and the American Federation of Television and Radio Artists. In Australia and New Zealand, actors' professional interests in all fields are looked after by Equity.

The unions also provide all kinds of useful services, such as insurance, tax advice, legal help and so on. Equity also publishes an informative magazine, distributed free to members.

The size of your contribution may vary according to your (voluntarily disclosed) income but it will not be expensive (Equity, for instance, sets a notional 1 per cent of annual income as the top voluntary contribution expected of its highest earners. Most of we lesser mortals pay what seems to me to be a reasonable amount – call the Equity head office for current rates.)

But is it easy to join an actors' union, and will it help your chances of finding work? The old 'Catch 22' which people used to quote, that 'You can't join Equity until you get a job and you can't get a job until you join Equity' never really was true, and it certainly isn't now. To start with, as already noted, membership of British Equity is granted automatically to graduates of accredited acting schools.

In North America Equity requires evidence of your having been offered a professional acting contract, or of previous professional experience totalling some 50 weeks' employment. SAG and AFTRA require evidence of your having been offered a professional contract in the media. All three unions operate a reciprocal agreement that a year's paid-up membership of one entitles you to membership of the other two, if required. In Australia and New Zealand, Equity requires you either to be in receipt of an offer of professional acting work, or to be a graduate of a recognized professional training course.

However, anybody can call themselves an actor and ask to be paid for their work, irrespective of whether or not they're in the union. Consequently, many fringe companies, which (almost by definition) can't afford to pay anything other than basic expenses, use actors who may not be members. But to work in recognized and reputable fringe theatres is now often looked upon as a *bona fide* qualification for union membership. It used to be that you couldn't have full Equity membership (and therefore were excluded from West End or television work) until you had 'notched up' 40 weeks' experience in regional repertory. These rules are now much more flexible: it's worth checking with the Equity office as to what is now considered relevant experience.

As already noted, in North America there is a long-established tradition in regional theatre of Equity members working alongside non-Equity members. However, for the sake of your own protection, you should always check the union status of any paid employment before you sign a contract. Many would say it is also a matter of professional ethics to do so.

As to whether or not union membership helps you get work, my response is, yes, in many cases. The fact that you have taken the trouble to assemble the professional experience and/or training to become an Equity member shows you have credentials as a responsible member of the trade. Many directors are themselves members, and most producers prefer to work in a professional framework, with recognised channels for sorting out disputes, agreed conditions of employment, etc.

■ Advertising. As a professional, **you need to advertise your wares**.

  ■ If you have an **agent**, her or his percentage is deductible from your income tax because she or he is being paid to promote your work for you. Part of her or his work is to distribute your details to casting directors, producers, etc. and thus the percentage you pay the agent is, in a sense, money spent on advertising.

  ■ **Photographs**. Your agent, and yourself, will need a good set of photographs to distribute. Shop around – many photographers advertise in *Back Stage*, *Contacts*, *The Stage*, etc. and on the notice-boards of places like the Actors' Centre. Many photographers offer special low rates to drama students and young actors. But good work costs money – by the time you've paid for multiple re-prints (and get a good size , 10″ × 8″ is what's expected) on top of the photographer's fee, you will need, at present prices, to set aside at least £200 (c.$350.) Even though your photograph may appear in a casting directory (see below) you must have your own supply in reserve.

■ **Casting directories**. At the time of going to press, the fee for a half-page advertisement for a year in *The Spotlight* is approximately £120. See below for the telephone numbers of American/Australian equivalent publications, to check their current rates. Other forms of advertising for actors are starting to develop – rumours of an Equity directory on the Internet, for example, so keep your ears open.

■ **World Wide Web**. Having said that, if you're on the **Internet** yourself, there's absolutely nothing to stop you designing and broadcasting your own web-site, letting potential employers know its address by e-mail.

■ **Printing, stationery**, etc. Even if you've got an agent, in the early days you will need to send out many photographs and CVs yourself, and so will need to budget for:

■ printing up and multi-copying **a clear, concise, curriculum vitae (or CV)**. Easily achieved in these days of home computers, so if you haven't got a PC, sweet-talk someone who has. Think carefully about the layout and content of this, as casting directors need to find out information about you quickly and easily. Feature your achievements and qualifications simply, and don't embellish, with, for instance, quotes from your local newspaper as to how moving they found your performance as Peer Gynt. If you are going to send in press quotes, send them in as separate photocopies – but only if you are quite certain they are relevant to the particular casting for which you are asking to be considered.

It's important to lay out your employment history with the most recent events first. But don't worry if you are just completing your training: a casting director will still need to see clearly laid out the parts you have played at drama school, and the names of any professional directors you worked with.

At the end of this section, I offer a sample CV of a mythical actor some two years out of drama school.

■ card-backed envelopes, so that your photographs don't get scrumpled up in the post.

■ postage stamps.

■ decent notepaper: included in 'Advertising' must be letter writing. You will need to work hard at garnering every scrap of information about who is casting what when (see below) and be ready to send off *short*, clear notes, accompanied by your brief, well-presented CV, and your uncluttered, $10'' \times 8''$ photograph, asking to be considered (preferably suggesting yourself for a specific part) and *briefly* explaining why you would be 'good casting'.

It is really self-defeating to send long letters, densely packed with chatty anecdotes about your Career So Far, and generously sharing your Philosophy of Acting. All, and I mean all, directors and casting directors are busy beyond belief and just want clear pictures and brief *facts*.

If you decide to invest in headed notepaper, make sure it is simple and unfussy. Nobody's going to be impressed by expensive corporate-style logos – your name and/or your address, simply and clearly set out, is all that is needed.

Once you have a relationship with a potential employer – i.e., when you have worked with them at least once – it is a good idea simply to keep in touch via postcards. Postcards from friendly acquaintances are pleasing things to get: from total strangers they are sometimes an irritant.

■ **Publications and casting information services**. There are various 'casting news-sheets', which seek to keep actors up to date with what's going on at the various studios and theatres. These casting sheets are quite expensive, so actors sometimes club together to subscribe (which the publishers try to discourage, but tough, many actors don't have much money). Some are also notoriously unreliable, and often are weeks or months late with information. However, I have to tell you that in the dim and distant past I myself found two jobs through the London Professional Casting Report, so maybe it's worth it. There are also nowadays 'casting information tapes' reachable via the telephone, for which you pay a high call charge, but remember, as with all payments for such services, this can be claimed for against tax: it's important to ask your telephone company for an itemised phone bill, on which you can identify your business calls.

The information at the end of the book includes a selection of casting information services.

■ Equity, and the other actors' unions, sometimes offer casting information services – check with head office.

■ Sympathetic receptionists at down-town rehearsal venues can often be persuaded to tell you who has booked the room for forthcoming auditions, and where to write to the director concerned. In fact, *Spotlight* run a tape-loop on a special telephone number for subscribers, saying who will be auditioning when at their premises.

■ Contact with casting directors. It's easy enough to find out how to contact independent casting directors – there are lists of offices in the publications listed below. Now, it's in the interest of casting directors to get to know actors, and many will spend some of their time each year interviewing newcomers. They will always ask you to 'keep in touch' and let them know when you are doing anything they can watch. Just be sensible in your subsequent relationship – don't pester needlessly, but do, in fact, 'keep in touch'. Most casting directors have assistants whose jobs include fielding calls from actors enquiring as to what films, plays, series, etc. their office will be dealing with in the near future, and will tell you if there's a part for which you might suggest yourself.

■ Similarly, the bigger theatre companies, like the RSC, the RNT, Manchester Royal Exchange, etc. have casting departments whose business it is to let the acting community know when casting is imminent, and will receive courteous and sensible enquiries from *bona fide* professionals seeking work. The same applies to casting departments at television companies, but you will find nowadays that much of the casting for television and films is 'farmed out' to independent casting directors (see above).

■ **Money management**. I am simply not equipped to provide detailed information as to the relationship which may exist between actors and tax systems throughout the English-speaking world, and so I here confine myself to a few observations on the current situation in the UK, and invite readers from elsewhere to make enquiries in their own countries. Most relevant trade unions will be able to provide information and advice.

In the UK, most performers pay income tax under Schedule D, i.e. at the end of the financial year. This may not be the case in other countries, and may, indeed, change in Britain – at the time of going to press there are rumours of the Government trying to alter the present relationship which actors have with the Inland Revenue and the Department of Social Services.

Actors historically in the UK have been able to pay tax as if they were self-employed, and yet could claim Unemployment Benefit between jobs as though they were regular workers made temporarily redundant. This situation is defendable on the grounds that actors have special skills and need always to be available in a fluid, changeable market-place. But it is undeniably a paradox, not always easy to explain, and often actors have difficulty in establishing a benefit claim at local offices where the officials are not used to dealing with theatricals. Consequently, actors traditionally 'signed on' at one or two central London benefit offices – Lisson Grove and Chadwick Street were two favourites – where their arrangements were known and understood. Nowadays, I understand the process is more streamlined, but, again, you should check with the Equity office as to what current legislation applies.

As regards tax, in the UK actors currently fall into the 'Self Assessment' category. In theory, you should be able to fill in all the tax forms yourself, and negotiate the amount you are liable to pay at the end of the year. My own experience is that to retain a good accountant with specialist knowledge is a sensible investment, who will prepare your tax return for you, and submit it to the tax office on your behalf, fielding any queries they have, and undertaking any negotiations which become necessary.

However, the accountant will need your help, in keeping a clear record of all payments you receive, all the paperwork that comes with them, plus receipts for all the things you can claim against your tax liability as legitimate expenses. This will include receipts for things like buying clothes and having them cleaned (known as 'care and replacement of wardrobe') and travel expenses to and from interviews and auditions, etc. The Equity office publishes a comprehensive list of what you can claim for, and also an informative booklet. Again, a very good reason for joining the Union.

A number of specialist accountants advertise in *The Stage* and at places like the Actors' Centre – but, as with agents, check their track record first. The Equity office will advise, as they keep a record of dodgy accountants. The risk with a dodgy agent is that they actually handle your money, and you need to be confident that they will hand over all payments due to you once they deducted their agreed percentage; with accountants, you have to be confident that their advice is sound. All freelance workers paying tax under Self Assessment are liable to be investigated every so many years. If the Inland Revenue decide you haven't been presenting your tax papers properly, and owe outstanding tax (or at worst, are liable to prosecution for Tax Avoidance) 'bad advice' from your accountant is not regarded as a legitimate excuse.

The **fees** accountants charge vary enormously, so once again check with either established colleagues or with the union as to what is a reasonable charge.

In countries which operate a **Value Added Tax system (VAT)** actors are regarded as part of a Service Industry, and if your annual turnover (i.e. your gross income) is above the VAT threshold you will then be drawn into the process of having to invoice all the companies which employ you for the VAT percentage payable over and above your fee, which you, at the end of the current tax quarter (three-month period) pass on to the government VAT office, minus all the VAT which you have already paid on services and purchases directly connected with your business practice as an actor. **Receipts have to be supplied**. In Britain, the VAT officers are part of the Customs and Excise service, quite separate from the Inland Revenue. While all the VAT officers I have dealt with have been perfectly fair-minded, their guidelines are much less flexible than those of their IR colleagues.

If you are liable for VAT, either make sure your accountant is equipped to advise you properly as to the system, or go and sit down with your local VAT collector as soon as you 'join', and make sure you're clear as to what is required of you. Always contact them if you are unsure as to procedure. As with the Inland Revenue, you will be liable for investigation every few years, and if Her Majesty's Custom and Excise decide you haven't been playing by their rules, you can be in Deep Trouble.

However, most actors, at least during the early years of their career, don't earn enough to warrant inclusion in the VAT system, so you probably won't need to worry about it – unless, of course, you rocket to stardom. But in this case you should be earning enough to pay fancy fees to posh lawyers and accountants to keep you well out of trouble. Having said that, a number of famous names over recent years have come awful croppers through bad advice, so even if you're making it big, make sure your professional advisors come with impeccable references from sources you know and respect.

Above all, you must cultivate the habit of **saving** a portion of all the money you are paid. This requires considerable will-power. If you've been out of work for a while, and have either been living off benefit or surviving on a pittance earned behind a bar, the arrival of a cheque for a few thousand pounds or dollars for a television or film job creates an almost unbearable temptation to Binge, and to Hell with the consequences. Take it from me, if only you can discipline yourself immediately to lock away at least a quarter – more prudent souls would say a third – of that cheque in a high-interest savings account you will be saving yourself a lot of angst at the end of the financial year when the taxman demands his due.

Chris Denys, the Principal of Bristol Old Vic Theatre School, tells his new students that, in choosing to become actors, they have chosen 'against growing up'. Well, yes, the freelance life, with its whiff of anarchy and apparent freedom from responsibilities does generate youthfulness, and some would argue even longevity, *but* the real world, alas, doesn't go away, and a flinty-eyed tax officer in a chilly room in the Euston Road is remarkably unsusceptible to theatrical charm and wit, be it ever so child-like.

While we're on savings: when you're 22 the idea of setting up a **pension scheme** may be way down your list of priorities. But again, try to be disciplined and clear-eyed enough to picture yourself 40 years hence with failing health and possibly with dependants (go on, use your Stanislavsky questions!) To start with even a low-payment scheme may well save you a lot of worry later on. At the risk of being boring, again, check with the Equity office, who will advise on flexible schemes which cope with the fluctuating nature of actors' ability to commit to regular payments.

On fame and other burdens

You will find in your chosen trade an amazing emotional landscape of mountains and troughs. In a word of advice to RADA leaving students in a Channel 4 documentary made some years ago, Sir John Gielgud exhorts them 'Try to keep working – and not to let either extreme success or extreme failure get to you.'

There will be times when you question your right to offer yourself as an actor – time and again you may see parts you know were virtually written to be played by you go to someone who is clearly quite unsuitable, and said by every one of your friends not to have a fraction of your talent. You may spend weeks and months when the only interviews your agent can get for you are for television commercials or industrial training videos, where the producers have not the slightest interest in your acting skills, merely in whether you 'look right'. (Swallow your pride – do all the commercials you can, as the money can be very useful – unless, of course, you have a moral problem with the 'product' e.g. some actors won't do military recruitment adverts.)

Then again, you may suddenly find yourself propelled from your inner-city bedsit to a glamorous location, where you are installed in a five-star hotel, become the focus of frantic press attention, and find yourself being whisked about in big cars to posh restaurants, receptions, press conferences, etc.

Always keep Sir John's Kiplinesque advice in mind: these demons of fame and of failure are but imposters. What matters is that you hang on to your sense of humour, and to your integrity as an honest craftsperson. The most famous actor in the world is still only an actor. If you're out of work, concentrate on maintaining your skills and your professional identity. If it's your turn to be famous this week, enjoy it, but always remember it's not important. It can be a darned nuisance – to be recognized the minute you step out of the front door has its drawbacks. People sometimes think they own you just because you appear on the box in their living room, and can be appallingly rude. I was once trapped at the checkout of a supermarket in Kentish Town while the till operator loudly berated me for appearing in 'that daft comedy series – I just can't stand it, you're all so stupid . . .' Hang on in there, don't get cross – it could be you working the till next month . . . .

One of the popular perceptions about actors is that they are especially bad at sustained personal relationships. I don't know if anyone has ever published any statistics to test this belief, but my observations over 30 years, for what they're worth, are as follows. While I can't see that workers in theatres and studios necessarily get into any more emotional and sexual muddles that those in shops and offices, for instance, I do recognize that there are some special conditions. Actors are often attractive people, whose looks and personality are part of their stock in trade, and who therefore tend to be much more 'up front' about presenting themselves to the world. Our craft involves using our bodies and our emotions, and thus emotions sometimes are much more 'available' than perhaps in an office concerned with say, geological surveying. We can probably all think of occasions when two people required to pretend to fall in love as part of a play end up getting involved in real life – Tom Stoppard's play *The Real Thing* explores this phenomenon brilliantly. Some areas of our work are glamorous and exciting, with perhaps attendant temptations to indulgence and debauchery, although as I've already hinted, most actors have a social life a far cry from the sex'n'drugs'n'rock'n'roll world which is supposed to exist in the world of entertainment.

The other side of all this is that, if an actor works diligently at the craft, exploring many different aspects of human behaviour, she or he will often achieve a considerable amount of self-knowledge, and become a 'well-balanced' person. As a result, some of the strongest long-term relationships I know are between couples involved in the acting profession. Obviously there will be pressures – especially early on, when tensions may arise as one partner achieves great success and the other doesn't. But I can think of many couples, both gay and heterosexual, who have managed to achieve many wonderfully fulfilling years of partnership.

Networking

In an earlier chapter, I listed some of the pubs, clubs, restaurants, etc. where actors often 'hang out'. These are often also places, of course, where directors, agents, etc. can be found. Once you've started to find a foothold as an actor, you may find it beneficial to frequent these places. Directors and the like are only human, and if they have a nodding acquaintance with you it's quite possible they might ask you to read for a production they may be working on.

Sometimes out-of-work actors make a point of meeting their more fortunate working chums for lunch or an after-rehearsal drink at, for instance, downtown rehearsal rooms, which sometimes have in-house catering. It's a commonly held belief that much casting is done through a particular actor being a familiar face in workplace canteens.

There's no statistical evidence, to my knowledge, that this kind of networking creates results – but if you've the stomach for it, you may feel that you're at least putting every effort into looking for work, and thus feel less frustrated than if you're just sitting at home waiting for the phone to ring.

I've never been much good at it. Once I was nearing the end of a theatre tour, and playing Canterbury, an hour or so's drive from London. I called a friend of mine who I knew was producing a series of one-off dramas at the BBC, to see if by chance there were any parts coming up I might be right for. 'Why don't you come on down to the Acton rehearsal rooms for lunch, and we'll have a chat?' said my good-hearted chum. It wasn't until I arrived in the canteen that I realized I was 'doing lunch at the BBC' – a notorious networking strategy. There were lots of actors there, in rehearsal for this and that. 'Hello, love, what are you in?' they all said 'Oh, just having lunch . . .' 'Oh, lunch, eh? Fine . . .' they all said, grinning knowingly. During lunch with my producer friend, a series of directors came over to our table to consult with him on various production points. Now my friend has never himself been an actor, but, as a very good friend, was determined to help me in every way he could. As each director arrived, he said 'Now, do you know Ellis Jones? Very interesting actor – looking for work at the moment . . .' This was, of course, tremendously kind, and was exactly why I was there, but my sensitive ego felt I might just have walked in with a cardboard sign saying 'Out-of-Work Thesp – any offers?' Anyway, after lunch I trundled off a bit sheepishly, feeling guilty that I wasn't as wholehearted in my appreciation of my pal's generosity as I should have been. I decided to call in on another friend who lived nearby, an actor who I hadn't seen for some time. As I drove up to his house, I noticed all the curtains were drawn. I rang on the doorbell. After a pause a figure appeared – unkempt, haggard, with three days' growth of beard. 'What's up? You look dreadful' I said. 'Come in Jones – I'm busy celebrating an anniversary' came the glum reply. 'Anniversary?' 'Yes, it's a full year to the day since I last had a job . . .' My guilt immediately quadrupled – I was at least still working at a theatre job – here was someone who at any time over the last many months would have killed to be introduced to television directors by a working producer.

The moral is, yes, you should network, you should put yourself about, but find a balance between being agreeable and being pushy, and, if you're not working, look as though you are . . .

Suggested further reading

How to be a Working Actor by James Duke (Virgin, 1994)

How to be a Working Actor by Henry and Rogers (Back Stage Books)

Making Acting Work by Chrys Salt (Bloomsbury, 1997)

The Actor's City Source Book (Back Stage Books, 1992)

DAISY ENWRIGHT
CURRICULUM VITAE

AGENT: DAVID MERRY ASSOCIATES, 14 James Lane, London, WC1 4BP.
Tel: 0171 333 4900   Fax: 0171 333 4911
Height: 5' 4"   **Hair**: blonde   **Eyes**: blue
Ethnic background: Caucasian, British
Playing age: 20 to 26

Stage:

Production	Character	Director
Since leaving drama school in 1997:		
HAMLET (Shakespeare),	OPHELIA	Tim Jones
Wolsey Theatre, Ipswich		
CABARET (Kander/Ebb) Tour	SALLY	Jane Smith
WEDGE (new play by Tom Block)	DORA	Vic Moss
fringe production at the		
Duke's Head, Bayswater		
At Wester Ross School of Acting (1994–7):		
HAPPY DAYS (Beckett)	WINNIE	Nick West
THARK (Travers)	KITTY	Liz Kane
HENRY VI (Shakespeare)	QUEEN MARGARET	Ken Hope
GLAD TIMES (Devised)	Jill/Waitress/ Socialworker	Jerry Stock

TV/Film:

CORONATION STREET – Girl in teashop (featured)		Rick Starr
Commercial for Westland Building Society		Tim Dewar

Radio/voice-over:
Presenter for Lampshire Hospital Radio

Singing range: soprano (to top C)
Dance: jazz, tap, classical, ballroom
Driving licence: (provisional)
Languages: French (fluent), Welsh (able to read)
Dialects: RP, Welsh, Cockney, East Anglia
Special skills: Horse-riding (expert)
Fight Proficiency Certificate (*Grade 1*)
Judo (brown belt)
Word-processing (WORD for Windows)
Experience before drama school: 1 year as trainee with a graphic design company

12 SURVIVING AS AN ACTOR – AND AS A HUMAN BEING

We keep coming back to the business of being realistic. The number of actors who make enough money to live well right from the start of their careers is tiny. You are likely to struggle for several years before you become established enough for your income from acting to attain any semblance of consistency, and even the most established stars will tell you there are times when they haven't a clue where the next job is coming from. Sometimes a young actor will rocket to stardom within a few months of leaving drama school, and for a few heady months will be really 'hot', being considered for all the juvenile leads in all the latest productions. Then another new hot property is discovered and suddenly the phone goes deadly quiet.

It is perfectly possible to have back-up sources of income while maintaining your own sense of self-respect, and without losing your identity as an actor. You may well also find it makes sense to have other creative outlets, as well as just acting – painting, or a musical activity, perhaps just as a hobby, for example – or a creative activity which could even supply extra income – such as picture-framing.

In terms of paid jobs which may fit with your agenda of needing to be free for auditions, etc. here are a few suggestions.

> ■ **Driving**. To have a clean driving licence is often useful. You can pick up casual delivery work via commercial and industrial employment agencies. If you own a four-door car, and have a good knowledge of your local area, you may consider offering yourself as a cab service, though I recognize that no London black cab driver will now ever speak to me again for having suggested it, and you may well find that the city in which you live has stringent laws preventing casual operators in this field. So check carefully first.

- **Office work**. Again 'temping' can be reasonably easily obtained via agencies, particularly if you live in a big city. These days, of course, you need at least word-processing skills, and it helps if you can cope with the more common database programmes. Short courses in these sorts of skills are reasonably priced, and there is usually a range of such courses at your local adult education office. Check at your local library.

- **Domestic skills**. If you're good with children, there are always families who need help with **child-care**, although my advice would be to spend some time acquiring training. Once again, legal restrictions may well be in place. Back to the library again. **House-cleaning** can be quite fun, and is arranged through agencies. Check Yellow Pages.

- **Working with food and drink**. 'Waiting tables' is a classic out-of-work actor's standby; in parts of California, if Equity or SAG suddenly banned its membership from working as waiters, the entire restaurant industry would collapse. Wages are low – sometimes you are expected to work purely for tips – so check out the restaurants with well-heeled clientele. Don't just plunge in – try to get some experience in a friendly environment before offering yourself to the Ivy or the Savoy Grill. It's tough work, and there are essential skills to be learned. Some actors go the whole hog and learn 'silver service', which raises your earning power quite a lot.

  Similarly, **working in bars** is tough, and badly paid unless you're in a high-tipping environment. As with silver service, if you're prepared to spend time learning to mix cocktails, you move into a better paid, and better-tipped, league.

  Cooking skills are always in demand, and some time spent learning to be, for instance, a commis chef (i.e. someone who does the 'dogsbody work' preparing and cleaning up for a fully qualified creative chef) can pay dividends. If you're really good at cooking, another idea is to set up your own party catering company – but in big cities like Sydney, New York, London, etc. this is now a fiercely competitive field, so study the potential market carefully first.

■ **Working in theatres and museums**. Some actors like to work as ushers, or as backstage staff, simply to stay in touch when they're not working as actors. Big theatres in big cities have a high turnover of staff, so it's worth asking to speak to the Front of House Manager at places like the National Theatre, or say, the Lincoln Centre, about foyer vacancies. Backstage work is often highly unionized; if you happen to have membership of a relevant union, like BECTU, you can sometimes pick up casual work, for instance on West End or Broadway shows, via the union office. Otherwise, simply go to the stage door and ask to speak to the Resident Stage Manager.

Some museums now use actors as part of the 'experience' on offer, and employ them to act out 'typical' scenes in a recreated historical environment – the Museum of the Moving Image on the South Bank in London is one such.

■ **Other suggestions**. There are, of course, dozens and dozens of ways to earn a buck. If you have strikingly good (or just striking) looks, you can try checking out the world of **modelling**. Model agencies are easy enough to find, and some actually advertise for clients in the acting trade publications, like *Back Stage*.

If you have a teaching qualification, you can ask to be put on your local education authority 'supply' (or temporary) **teaching** list, although in Britain I believe day-to-day supply teaching is much less of the norm, and you may be asked to give an undertaking of being available for a whole term at a time. Teaching English as a Foreign Language pays well, and time and money spent gaining a TEFL qualification is worthwhile. If you live in an area with a lively **tourist industry**, you may find it worthwhile to train as an official **guide** (in Britain the 'BlueBadge' qualification awarded by the London Transport Board is a respected benchmark, and opens the door to quite remunerative work, especially during the summer months). If you're good at DIY, the **building and decorating** trades are often sources of casual work.

In summary, in order to survive you need money, and in order to survive reasonably well you may well need another marketable skill or qualification to back up your talent and your training as an actor. The trick is not to lose touch with your identity as a performer – if you find a reasonably well-paid, reliable 'back-up' job, you may suddenly wake up one day to find you've become a career teacher, bar manager, computer programmer or whatever. Keep writing those letters, keep going to classes, set yourself the task of learning a new audition speech every week, keep practising your skills. If you have the time and are particularly good at sight-reading, recording **books for the blind** is a good way to keep those particular skills in trim: some organizations will pay you, others are voluntary. The contact organizations for actors with disabilities at the end of this book will be able to help in this area.

Feeding your talent – further training

Several times in this book I've mentioned the need to keep practising the craft. In a trade which is by its nature intermittent, at least for the majority of actors, maintaining and developing your reflexes as a performer is really important. Other performance artists, such as singers and dancers, automatically include training and practice in their agendas, so why on earth don't actors?

There is, at last, a shift in culture: increasingly British actors are picking up their cue from American and European colleagues, and 'taking class' when they're between jobs, or even when they're working. A long run in the West End, for instance, can create a wonderful opportunity to develop new skills – and the cash to pay for tuition.

In North America, *Backstage* (which has editions for both New York and the West Coast) carries pages of adverts for training of all kinds, and every so often runs special supplements; in Australia and New Zealand, keep in touch with *Lowdown* and its spin-off *Directions*. In London, *The Stage* carries several pages of training advertisements every week, and the Equity journal will have details of refresher courses on offer to professional actors at the various drama schools.

You can keep in touch with all of these via the list at the end of this book.

I am a great believer in the Actors' Centre movement: there are Actors' Centres in Britain, North America and Australia. Oddly enough, they are not related in any sense other than they share a common purpose of providing support for professional actors, in terms of classes, workshops, social contacts, information exchange and creating opportunities for acting work. There are, of course, other places where actors meet (in New York, for instance, the various entertainment unions have 'lounges' where their members can meet socially) but for the purposes of this book I shall simply list at the end of this book the Actors' Centres, where you will no doubt be able to find details of other facilities available to professional actors in your region.

EPILOGUE: BEYOND THE CD-ROM

As the Age of Technology progresses, the actor faces new challenges and doubtless more will emerge in the new millennium. In the early 1970s, I was one of the first actors in the UK to become regularly involved with 'blue screen' television – Colour Separation Overlay, or Chroma-Key. In the children's magic sitcom for Thames Television, *Pardon My Genie*, in which I played a latter-day Aladdin, all kinds of tricks were achieved by separating out the blue channel from the master shot on one camera, and mixing in a shot taken with a second camera of a person or an event filmed with an all-blue background. There would be no blue anywhere on the master set and the pictures from the two cameras would merge. So, for example, an actor could appear to have shrunk to pixie-size simply by shooting him on the second camera with a long-shot lens, and mixing into the first camera's picture which would be framing, say, a horse, in medium close-up. The seemingly tiny actor could then appear, with a bit of carefully organized mime, to appear to be climbing out of the horse's ear.

Versions of this technique have now reached high levels of sophistication: the film of *The Borrowers*, for example, has some amazing effects. The new technology allows the principle of blue-screen to be used in three dimensions and actors can be filmed in virtual sets, which exist only in a computer program.

We can but speculate on the effect these changes will have. For years, actors have had to learn to react to effects in film and television drama which are added in their absence, in the editing suite, but this is something else. Entire dramas can now be created with the actors moving on a neutral (or blue, sometimes yellow) set with only a few props and odd pieces of furniture, and entire worlds – buildings, landscapes, animals – added to the action electronically.

More disturbingly, an actor's entire performance can now be created electronically, simply by sampling his or her image and vocal quality and manipulating the vision and sound in a computer. Long-dead stars can now give performances in films scripted by writers born years after the actors concerned departed. The television commercial in which the late Steve McQueen appeared to drive a 1998 Ford around San Francisco was apparently achieved by manipulating some shots lifted from the 1960s film *Bullitt*.

But they'll never replace live actors, will they . . . ? Were there people at the turn of the nineteenth century saying 'But they'll never replace the horse and cart, will they . . . ?' The great designer and theatre sage, Edward Gordon Craig, in the early years of the twentieth century, had a vision of the actor being replaced by a Super Marionette, infallible, unsusceptible to human frailty. Perhaps Craig's dream is now being realized in a Quantel Editing suite somewhere in California. I comfort myself with the fact that even if film and television dramas become entirely the domain of electronically generated images, people will still want to act and will still create stages and theatres. Audiences will always want to experience sharing a journey through a story at the same time and in the same place as the performers.

Perhaps the Age of New Technology will also be the Age of the New Theatre Renaissance, who knows? Certainly in the UK, there are new theatres being built with money from the National Lottery and perhaps money may even be found to put productions into them.

What will never change is human instinct. The instinct to perform, to impersonate, to show off, to sing and to dance, to act out stories will always be there. The great works of dramatic literature are indestructible and the special magic of being in the presence of a major acting talent, as they take you on their journey through a great play, can exist only in terms of real people and only in the 'now'; even the most realistic recording will always be a recording, be it never so digital, be it never so virtual.

Crystal ball gazing is a futile exercise: when Sir Herbert Beerbohm Tree founded his Academy of Dramatic Art in 1904, he little thought that its graduates would, by the end of the century, be packaging their work in little discs, roughly the size of the saucers in Lady Tree's bone china tea-service. If the Vice-Principal of RADA feels moved to write a book about acting in 2098, I daresay the CD-ROMs and virtual reality sets which intrigue us at the moment will look to her or him much as penny-farthing bicycles look to us now.

We at RADA are currently charged by the Arts Council of England with using National Lottery funds to create 'an Academy of Dramatic Art for the twenty-first century and beyond'. Actors will continue to seek training, whatever form the media may take, and tutors will find ways to teach them. We are talking about the human spirit's irrepressible need to express itself and to achieve excellence in that expression.

Meanwhile, good luck in your endeavours to find a place in the world of acting as it now exists – I hope you've found some useful pointers in this book. And if you find great success and riches, or if the business sometimes leaves you in near despair, never forget, it's only a play . . .

THE LANGUAGE OF THE TRADE

Assuming that, having picked up some of the social buzz around the theatre scene, you decide actually to get involved, it's as well to know the language. So here follow some of the expressions you might come across. You can always stock your bookshelf with one or two more comprehensive 'cribs' such as the theatre volume of *Bluff Your Way in . . .* books, but the following should serve reasonably well.

Absurd, Theatre of a phrase invented by Martin Esslin in the 1960s to encapsulate a genre of plays which developed when the world seemed to be doomed by the shadow of the Bomb, commenting obliquely (and sometimes very wittily and poetically) on the absurdity of human existence; writers usually quoted in this context are Ionescu, Pinter, Beckett and N. F. Simpson

actor, actress it's worth noting that, of late, it's become rather non-politically-correct to use the word 'actress', which in some circles is categorized with calling women 'ladies' or 'girls'; the term 'female actor' is now the accepted phrase

actor-manager in common with other professions, people who achieve success like to be in control; there must always have been actors who were also managers – Shakespeare, for instance, was a major shareholder at the Globe, but the term 'actor-manager' usually refers to the leading lights of the eighteenth and nineteenth century touring and London companies: Garrick, Foote, Sheridan in the eighteenth, Kemble, Tree, Irving, Benson in the nineteenth and early twentieth, and later examples are Wolfit, Olivier and Branagh

ad-lib making it up as you go along, often because you can't think of the next line to save your life; some actors are brilliant at it, there are myths of old Shakespearian hands who could extemporize in blank verse – not to be confused with 'devised theatre' (q.v.)

alternative theatre   *see* fringe

apron stage   a proscenium-arch stage, extending out into the auditorium; this developed in England during the late sixteenth and early seventeenth century and, for a time, was a popular place for the young blades in the audience to sit

arena theatre   one with an open acting area, almost 'in the round' (the term comes from the Latin for 'sand' and thus presumably harks back to the days of amphitheatres, Christians for the throwing-to-lions-of); a number of impressive arena theatres were built in the 1960s and 1970s, notably Stratford in Ontario, the Olivier Theatre in London, the Crucible at Sheffield, the Guthrie Theatre in Minneapolis and the Festival Theatre at Chichester

arc-light   an early form of spotlight

aside   a line played directly to the audience, supposedly not in the hearing of the other characters onstage; used a lot, for instance, in Restoration and eighteenth-century comedy

ASM   assistant stage manager

audition   literally, a 'hearing' of how well a prospective actor may speak his or her lines; in practice it can mean anything from a formal reading to a group improvization to a full-scale, learn-it-on-the-spot song and dance routine

backstage   behind the scenes; 'to go backstage' after the show is still a tradition amongst actors and friends of actors, which some actors don't like – there's always the bother of being caught in your vest with your beard half off – and may well prefer to meet you in the bar

barndoor   a flap on the side of a spotlight, used to restrict the spread of the beam

batten   literally, a length of wood; sometimes used to strengthen scenery, or sometimes a row of stage-lights is called a batten

blacks   sometimes a play may be performed 'in front of blacks' – in other words, with just plain black drapes in place of scenery; 'blacks' can also refer to clothing – a black top and black tights or jeans – and some companies of actors perform simply in blacks to throw focus onto the text: most stage managers and stage crew have a set of blacks in their wardrobe for moving props and scenery during stage blackouts (q.v.)

blackout when a play, or a scene from a play finishes, and the lights 'fade to black'; in Britain, fire regulations require at least discreet lighting to indicate where the exits are, so a complete black-out is almost impossible to achieve. (There is a joke about the theatre stage manager who dies, and on arrival at the Pearly Gates, is asked by St Peter if there's a special request he would like granted now he's arrived in Paradise. The stage manager immediately requests a complete and absolute blackout, something he'd never achieved on earth. St Peter obliges and the entire universe is plunged into darkness for a whole minute. When the lights come up again St Peter blinks and asks 'Where are my Pearly Gates?' Triumphantly the stage manager cries 'I've just struck 'em!' Oh, sorry – *see* **strike**.)

blocking basically, what dancers call choreography – sorting out who stands where when, and when they move, and where they move to; traditionally, the director's job, but sometimes companies work democratically, letting the blocking arrive naturally. (Personally, I think you need someone to make the final decision and that it's part of the director's craft to develop a feel for effective blocking. Peter Hall is brilliant at it.)

book in musical plays, the libretto is referred to as 'the book'; to be 'on the book' in stage-management terms, means to be the prompter. This job is usually undertaken by the DSM (q.v.)

border a strip of material hanging above the stage, used in proscenium theatres to complete the 'frame' of the stage picture and/or to 'mask' the flown stage-lighting

Boulevard theatre popular French plays – often melodramas – of the late eighteenth and nineteenth centuries

bowdlerised scripts plays which have been badly rewritten, or cut, or distorted in some way; refers to the good doctor Thomas Bowdler, who edited Shakespeare in the late eighteenth/early nineteenth century cutting out all the rude bits

break a leg nobody seems to know why American actors use this expression instead of wishing someone good luck on their opening night; I've asked many transatlantic pros, and received various historical explanations, not all of which sound terribly convincing. My favourite is anecdotal. It seems that John Wilkes Booth, having fired the shot which killed President Lincoln during a performance at New York's Ford's

Theatre in 1865, leapt from a box in the auditorium on to the stage – and, in so doing, broke his leg. Nonetheless, he managed to escape and was not captured until some 12 days later. Since Booth was an actor by trade, one can see the link. Well, sort of.

Broadway   the Great White Way of New York theatre-land; in fact, most of the Broadway theatres are in streets dissecting Broadway itself in the area around Times Square – the term 'off-Broadway' refers to the smaller theatres in the area, which often present adventurous and experimental work, as do the 'off-off Broadway' theatres in other parts of the city, (e.g. in Greenwich Village)

business   any activity undertaken during the course of the performance involving gesture or the handling of props may be referred to as stage business, or 'biz'; some comedy actors develop 'business' which becomes part of their stock in trade. (A rather down-trodden theatre manager appeared backstage after a performance of *A Midsummer Night's Dream* in a London theatre, offering to employ all of the actors playing the 'mechanicals' in a tour he was hoping to mount, starring a well-known comic: 'We won't have much time for rehearsal, lads – bring your own biz . . .'

calls   at the end of each day's rehearsal, the director gives the stagemanager the actors' 'calls' for the next day – in other words, what time they're supposed to turn up for rehearsal; during runs of performances in the theatre, the actors are all expected to be at the theatre for the half-hour call (usually just called 'the half') 35 minutes before curtain up, or half an hour before the 'beginners call' which is at five minutes before curtain-up. The stage manager is responsible for making sure the actors receive a 'quarter-hour call' and a 'five-minute call' during the half-hour leading up to 'beginners'. (In the old variety theatres, a 'call-boy' would be employed.) Sometimes actors will be given calls during the course of the performance, a few minutes before their next entrance – but all actors have to recognize that this is a courtesy service, and that they are always responsible for appearing onstage at the right time!

camp   a word no longer exclusively theatrical, it's used to describe what used to be called 'effeminate' behaviour or performance (also over-fussy or over-the-top design, or costume)

commedia dell'arte   a style of theatre which developed in Italy in the sixteenth century but with roots going right back to Roman times; stock characters (Pantalone, Arlecchino, etc.), basic storylines giving lots of room for improvisation, sometimes studied at drama schools, sometimes a source and inspiration for 'experimental' theatre

community theatre   loose term, including productions put on in schools, factories, in market places, often dealing with social 'issues'; 'community plays' are projects involving large numbers of non-professional performers, sometimes led by a professional director and/or writer – there are professional companies who specialize in producing large-scale theatrical events involving communities: one such is Welfare State International, who are based in Cumbria

corpse   used as a verb, 'to corpse' means to giggle in the middle of a performance – unforgivable

costume   even if your part requires you to wear modern jeans and shirt, your clothes onstage or on camera will still be called your 'costume'. Camp actors have been known to refer to their 'cossie' or even their 'frock'

cue   there are two kinds, actors' cues and technical cues; your acting cue is the line spoken by a fellow performer immediately before your line (old-fashioned actors, if they couldn't remember their next line, would call out to the prompter, 'cue!'); technical cues are the ones given by the stage-manager to the crew onstage, sometimes with a system of signal-lights, sometimes verbally over an intercom

Actors are sometimes given **cue-lights** if they have to make an entrance the cue for which is non-verbal – for instance, a piece of business hidden from the actor by scenery. The stage-manager will flash the light – usually a low-wattage single blue bulb (blue light is less noticeable than white light)

curtain   in proscenium arch theatres, the front curtain is always referred to as the 'tabs'; the stage manager's cue call for bringing down the curtain is 'Tabs, go!' (They're called tabs because at one time there was a fashion for the actors to 'freeze' at the end of a scene into a 'tableau vivante' on which the curtain was lowered)

dark   a theatre which is closed and has no shows to offer the public is referred to as being 'dark'

devised theatre   plays which have been developed in rehearsal, usually in a collaboration between actors and a director/writer; the roots of this obviously go right back to commedia (q.v.) and beyond (a celebrated modern practitioner of this artform, in both films and theatre, is a RADA graduate, Mike Leigh)

director   what's the difference between a producer and a director? In the 'straight' theatre and in films/television, the producer puts the whole business deal together, starting with raising the money, and going on to assemble the artistic and technical teams. The director directs the actors, and co-ordinates all the creative work. (Just to confuse matters, opera companies sometimes call the director the producer and, until recently, all radio drama was 'produced' rather than directed)

DLP   'dead letter perfect' – to know your lines completely accurately

downstage, upstage   *see* stage directions

dresser   technically, someone who is paid simply to help an actor put on and take off his/her costume; but dressers often develop into 'personal assistants', and many theatre stars have a dresser who has been with them for years

dress rehearsal   well, you know what a dress rehearsal is; actors usually call it just 'the dress'

dressing room   where you put on your costume before the play; not, note, a *changing* room – that's where you put on your shorts to play rugby

drying, to dry   to forget your lines

eye-line   what you see, or rather what the audience thinks you see, if you look straight in front of you; an actor's eye-line is particularly important to film editors

fishpole   in films and television, a hand-held pole with a microphone at one end and a sound technician at the other

flat   the essential building-block of traditional scenery – a wooden frame covered in canvas, which has had 'size' sloshed over it, then painted. (Size is a sort of glue, which helps the paint adhere better, and shrinks the canvas onto the frame, to form a taut surface. Size has an unmistakable smell, in my opinion far more evocative of life backstage than any stick of greasepaint.) Conventional flats are held in place by **stage braces**, which in turn are stopped from wobbling by **stage weights**, small square or cylindrical blocks of solid metal

flies, flying   the space above a conventional pros-arch stage is called 'the flies'; if the space is big enough to haul up full-size flats, it's called a **fly-tower**. Scenery which can be hauled up and down is called 'flown scenery'. Sometimes actors are called upon to simulate literal flying, as in *Peter Pan*; this is done by concealing a harness under the actor's costume and then hauling him/her through the air on a system of supposedly invisible wires

follow spot   a spotlight used to highlight a particular performer by following him/her around the stage, making sure he/she is surrounded by a circle of light; much used in ballet and musical theatre

Fresnel spotlight   a spotlight with a semi-opaque, diffused lense

fringe theatre   in Britain, theatre produced outside the mainstream of the West End or the traditional subsidized houses; the term began to be used in the early 1960s in Edinburgh, at the Traverse Theatre, which became the centre for a repertoire of plays alternative to the conventional fare officially on offer at the International Festival. The term spread to London with the establishment of the (now defunct) Arts Lab in Drury Lane and the growth of the London equivalent of off-Broadway and off-off Broadway in 'theatre spaces' (very often either basements or upper rooms in public houses)

front of house   the public area of the theatre – the foyer, etc.; usually shortened to FOH

get-in, get-out   the arrival and departure process for the scenery and props to and from theatres when a production is on tour; in large touring theatres this has to be carefully costed by the management as it often involves employing extra casual labour. The term **get-out** is also used to describe the minimum box-office take required to cover a production's cost

ghost – when the ghost walks   an expression still used by older actors to refer to payday; it's supposed to go back to the days when actors were paid in cash and was a kind of code to disguise the fact that on paydays the manager was carrying large quantities of (very vulnerable) cash

greasepaint   the form in which most stage make-up appeared until quite recently. Sticks of greasepaint have been made by the Leichner company since the mid nineteenth century. (A male actor's 'base' would usually be a mixture of Leichner sticks numbers 5 and 9.)

green room   the actors' rest-room backstage, traditionally green because green is reckoned to be most restful of colours; in fact, most green rooms aren't green – often they're notable for tea-stained sofas and brimming ashtrays – but they're still called green rooms

grid   the framework from which the lighting and scenery bars are hung above the stage (a traditional trick played on green-horn ASMs on their first day at work is to dispatch them up the fly-tower ladder to 'fetch the key to the grid' which, of course, doesn't exist)

ground-plan   as soon as a design for a production is finalized, the designer will supply scale copies of its basic outline to the director, lighting designer and stage manager, as well as, of course, to the construction team, then he/she will also supply the construction team with an accurate scale model of the set, often with working drawings as to how, particularly, sections are to be built

house   actors often refer to the audience as 'the house' – 'How's the house?' means how many are there in the audience, and what are they like?

iron   the fire-curtain, which in larger proscenium houses has to be test-dropped at least once when there is an audience in the building; this is usually done at the interval. (Some of the older fire-curtains are actually made of metal and are enormously heavy, requiring substantial – and often noisy – machinery. Emlyn Williams capitalizes on this in a play set in a theatre – *A Murder Has Been Announced* – in which the main character goes mad in the last scene, and is crushed by the descending fire curtain)

lighting   this has its own arcane vocabulary, much relished by practitioners, both amateur and professional – one or two of the most common types of stage lights are listed in this glossary, and in the world of film and television, you will find a more exotic range of names (three of my favourites are 'blondes', 'redheads' and 'pups'. You don't need to know which is which, just nod knowledgeably when the lighting director says 'You need to tilt your head up a bit, my son, I'm covering you with that blonde over there . . .')

mark out   in a rehearsal room, the stage management team will use the designer's ground-plan of the set to create an accurate outline on the floor, showing the actors clearly where the walls, windows, doors, etc. are

mask   obviously the noun 'mask' is self-evident, but it's also used as a verb in the theatre; 'to mask' something is to hide it from the audience's view – one of the points of arranging blocking is to avoid crucial bits of the action being masked

masque   a form of entertainment highly popular amongst European aristocrats and royalty during the early part of the seventeenth century; it had developed from the street processions of medieval times and included singing, dancing and acted scenes, with characters often disguised by masks. From the court masques developed opera and ballet, and many staging and design ideas which were absorbed into dramatic theatre. The most famous collaborators in this form were the architect/designer Inigo Jones and the playwright Ben Jonson

master carpenter　the term 'master' in terms of craft skills obviously derives from the medieval guilds and is still in use in the theatre world to denote seniority in the areas of scenery, prop making and wardrobe. Hence master carpenter, property master and wardrobe master or mistress. I've not heard the expression 'mistress carpenter', not yet anyway. In the West End, the Master Carpenter is the chief of the backstage team employed directly by the theatre itself (as opposed to those employed by the production company actually producing the play, who may have hired the use of the building) and is sometimes referred to as the Permanent Stage Manager, not to be confused with the Company Stage Manager (*see* stage management)

matinee　a 'daytime' as opposed to an evening performance – usually, to confuse French-speakers, in the afternoon; even more confusingly, West End and Broadway shows sometimes present special 'midnight matinee' performances for charity

melodrama, melodramatic　strictly speaking, melodrama is a style of theatre developed in France in the late eighteenth century in which actors spoke their lines to music; nowadays it's usually used as a pejorative term, referring to exaggerated and unconvincing displays of emotion

method acting　an approach to rehearsal developed by a director called Lee Strasberg at the Actors' Studio in New York in the 1950s, drawing on Strasberg's interpretation of Stanislavsky's (q.v.) writings – discussed elsewhere in this book, the most significant (and notorious) feature of The Method is the striving for 'emotional truth' by delving deep into your own 'emotional memory'

off the book　to know your lines well enough not to need to carry the script in rehearsal; the director will sometimes decree, for instance, that all the cast be 'off the book' by the end of the first week's rehearsal (in film, on the other hand, it's often useful to turn up 'off the book', in case it's a matter of 'turn up and turn over')

O.P.　*see* prompt

pageant　a type of spotlight used in theatres

panatrope　*see* sound

pantomime　most Brits know vaguely that a 'panto' is a show you are dragged along to at Christmas-time when you're a kid. Usually these days the stars are well known from television – although not necessarily as actors. Sometimes they're famous television presenters, or sports people. The 'traditional' pantomime will include a 'Principal boy' – played by a girl, and a 'Dame' – played by a man. The roots go back through the French eighteenth century Arlequinade theatre, through Italian commedia to Roman times. Most modern pantos are pretty grim, but you can still get a really good taste of gutsy popular theatre at its best in some regional theatres. The Glasgow Citizens' Theatre, for instance, still prides itself on its own home-grown Scottish version

perch   a bracket placed at the side of the stage, or on the walls of the auditorium, from which a spotlight is hung

Walter Plinge   the name traditionally used by managements in cast lists as a tongue-in-cheek 'disguise' when an actor is playing more than one part

plot   as well as the term for a play's storyline, this is also used for the list of technical cues kept in the prompt copy by the stage manager; thus there is a sound plot, and an 'lx' (lighting) plot. Usually during the pre-production set-up period time is set aside for a 'plotting rehearsal'

producer   *see* director

prompt, prompter   usually the DSM, described as being 'on the book'; the DSM also 'runs the show' – i.e. gives all the technical operators their cues, as well as being on stand-by to call out a line to an actor if he or she 'dries'. The DSM will have been on the book all the way through rehearsals and will know any areas where an actor's grasp of the words might be shaky. In a proscenium theatre the prompter will sit on one side of the stage, in 'the corner'. In arena theatres the cues are controlled from a control-room or area somewhere at the back of the audience and God help the actor if he dries

prompt-side   the side of the stage where the prompt-corner is found; traditionally, in Britain this is stage left and the stage right side is called **OP – opposite prompt**. Some people insist on calling stage right OP even when the prompter's desk is on the right-hand side. In America, the opposite is true

props   short for 'stage properties', meaning any object used in the play, from a cutlass to a handbag. Props kept by the actor in the dressing room and carried on by him/her as part of the action are called 'personal props'. Many a young actor is surprised when the stage manager appears in the dressing room during the 'half' with the request 'May I check your personals . . .?'

proscenium arch   in classical times the space 'before the scene' was called the *pro-skeneum* (In Roman and early Renaissance theatres there was often a permanent 'scene' which formed an all-purpose backing, like the one still in existence at Vicenza); thus, as the 'picture-frame' stage developed, the 'frame' became known as the proscenium arch

raked stage   traditional proscenium arch theatres often have a stage with a gentle (or sometimes not so gentle) slope, known as the 'rake', to improve sight lines (q.v.)

received pronunciation, or RP   otherwise known as 'standard English'; rather than squeeze out regional accents, we teach RP at RADA these days as a dialect to be learned alongside your native way of speaking

repertory, repertoire   a **repertory** theatre is one where plays are presented serially, one after another – there are still a very few remaining 'weekly reps' where a new play is presented every week; the more usual turnaround is three or four weeks. A **repertoire** theatre is one where several productions are kept in storage and are presented in rotation; the RSC and the RNT both operate this system

resting   an expression the general public seems to think professional actors employ as a euphemism for being out of work. In thirty years I've never heard an actor use it; we always say, 'Well, it's a bit quiet at the moment', or 'I'm on the dole', or quite simply, 'Since you ask, I'm out of bloody work, love . . .'

scenery   here are a few terms which sometimes confuse newcomers:

set – short for setting: the thing in which and in front of which you act; **box-set** – one showing the interior of a room, with the 'fourth wall' i.e. the one nearest the audience, missing; **flat** – the key component in traditional box-set scenery, canvas stretched over a wooden frame; **stage brace**   a bracket hooked to the back of a flat to hold it upright; **French flat** – a flat designed to be 'flown'(*see* flying); **French brace** – a wooden bracket fixed to the back of a flat for the same purpose; **border** – a strip of black cloth usually hung above the stage to 'mask' the lighting equipment; **barrel, or bard** – a metal pole from which scenery is 'flown' (*see* 'flying'); **lighting bar, or barrel** – as above but containing electric wires and connectors: the flying bars are numbered from the front of the stage back, i.e. downstage numbers first; **return** – a piece of scenery attached to the side of a flat to give it depth, in other words to create a three-dimensional appearance; **tormentor** – a 'neutral' piece of scenery (usually a plain black flat) used to narrow down the width of the stage picture, placed between the edge of the set and the proscenium frame

(*Also see* stage directions)

setting line   in a pros-arch theatre, an invisible line a few feet upstage of the pros which forms the 'base line' for the set; in other words, all the scenery is erected upstage of the setting line

sight lines, or lines of sight   how good a view your seat has of the stage depends on the 'sight lines' – in other words, is there anything interrupting a straight line between your eyes and the actor on the stage? This is an important element in the director and designer's preparation of a production

slapstick   derives from the floppy split stick which Arlequino carried in commedia plays; nowadays it's any form of broad, physical comedy

sound   sound effects today can, of course, be provided by highly effective, hi-tech kit. Stage managers used to give the cue, 'Pans, go'. This referred to the twin-turntable record-player called a panatrope which used to be used, in my stage-management days, to provide the music and sound. (I once had to sing onstage accompanying myself on the Welsh harp, which involved miming along to recorded harp chords played on the panatrope. On the first night I suddenly developed a prolonged coughing fit to disguise the repeated 'scrurch, scrurch . . .' emanating from the stage speakers, as the needle firmly lodged itself in a scratch on the record)

stage   you know what a stage is, but here's a summary of different types:

end stage – usually in a rectangular theatre, with the stage simply a platform at one end; **pros arch stage** – as above, but with a proscenium arch to create a picture frame; **apron stage** – as above, but with a section below the setting line which can be used as a playing area both when the curtain is in and when it's out. In Restoration and eighteenth-century theatres there is often a door (with sometimes a 'window' above it) on either side of the apron; **thrust stage** – a theatre with a stage extending from an end stage out into the auditorium. Most Elizabethan theatres seem to have been variants of this; **arena stage** – a theatre which has a basically circular, or oval shape, with the stage occupying a more-or-less central area, but incorporating an end-stage element, thus allowing flying, access to wing-space, etc. The RNT Olivier Stage in London is a classic example; **in-the-round staging** – where the audience sits all the way round, with the actors either making entrances along aisles in gaps in the seating, or through 'vomitories' – entrances leading to corridors under the auditorium. There are splendid examples at Stoke-on-Trent and Scarborough, both pioneered by the late Stephen Joseph

stage directions   the bits in a script when a playwright indicates what he/she would like to happen in terms of physical action to accompany the dialogue. If these are changed or added to in rehearsal, the changes are logged in the prompt copy by the DSM (q.v.). The terminology used is based on right and left as perceived by the actor as he or she faces the audience. (If you're playing in the round, the director usually makes an arbitrary choice as to which way is 'upstage'.) On a pros arch stage, upstage is the direction away from the audience, downstage towards it. Downstage left is the area left of the actor as he faces the audience, 'below' the centre-stage area. You can work all the variations out for yourself – upstage left centre, offstage right, etc.

stage managers   the function of these vital folk is discussed elsewhere in this book. Basically the stage management team organizes all the practical aspects of performance. In traditional theatre companies, there is an SM, sometimes also doubling as CSM (Company Stage Manager, who has administrative as well as practical responsibilities). Next in seniority is the DSM (Deputy Stage Manager) who usually creates the vital prompt copy during rehearsals, which not only is used for prompting the actors if they forget their lines, but also contains all the lighting and sound cues, actors' calls, etc. There is usually an ASM (Assistant Stage Manager) who has lots of jobs, including responsibility for assembling the necessary props, making sure the actors know their rehearsal calls, etc.

Stanislavsky, Constantin   Director of the Moscow Art Theatre during the 1890s and well into the twentieth century; chiefly famous for (a) directing the first productions of most of Chekhov's masterpieces, including *The Cherry Orchard* and *Uncle Vanya*, and (b) writing a number of books and essays about the nature of acting, the effects of which are discussed elsewhere in this book

stock companies   A term used in America for permanent repertory companies, with the same group of actors presenting a series of plays. Back in the eighteenth and nineteenth centuries, the term referred to permanent troupes of actors, each of whom had a specific function in acting out the stories of the plays. Thus, you had the Tragedian, and Low Comedian, the Ingenue, Walking Gentleman, etc. (The latter always had a small part in a production.)

strike   to take down the scenery

superstitions   I suppose because acting is such a precarious trade, actors have a host of traditional superstitions against misfortune. British actors wish each other 'Good luck' before a show, sending cards to each other on opening nights. A popular good luck message is 'May you have a big hand on your opening . . .' American actors believe it's actually bad luck to wish someone good luck, if you see what I mean, and so, perversely, exhort colleagues to 'break a leg' (q.v.). Presumably, this indicates a national pessimism concerning the perversity of Fate, but that's far too deep a topic to be confronted here. There are many superstitions: no fresh flowers onstage – presumably in case any of the company (or audience in the front few rows) suffers from hayfever; if the script calls for a Bible, it should be a book made to look like a Bible rather than the real thing – this may be linked to early clerical disapproval of the frivolous nature of theatre and goes back to the days when actors couldn't be buried in consecrated ground; the most famous theatrical superstitions are linked to Shakespeare's *Macbeth*. This play, including as it does supernatural characters and events, is supposed to be dogged with a history of misfortune. The most famous example of this in recent years was a production at the Old Vic theatre in London starring Peter O'Toole, which attracted the most atrocious reviews. Ironically, it became a cult hit and sold out completely in London and on tour. You're not supposed to mention the play by name, and an even worse sin is to quote it (unless, of course, you happen to be rehearsing or performing *Macbeth* itself, when you have no choice!) (On my first day working in the professional theatre, aged 17, I mentioned the title of the play, instead of using the accepted phrase, 'The Scottish Play'. I was hustled out to the stage door, made to spit, swear and knock on the door asking to be let back in. No kidding)

tabs   on a proscenium stage, the main curtain at the front which is raised at the start of the performance and lowered between acts; the expression comes from the French *tableau vivant*, referring to the stage picture revealed as the curtain rose

TIE   Theatre In Education; the idea of creating theatre especially for schoolchildren really developed during the 1960s, and some exciting companies now exist in many parts of the world

thespian   the origin of this rather arch term for a theatrical practitioner is the name of an ancient Greek, Thespis, who is supposed to have been the first chorus member (in the religious rituals of his day) to have split off from the others and claimed a solo spot, thus inventing acting

trap   trap-doors of various forms can still be found in old theatres, used to provide special effects in pantos, melodramas, etc, or, more passively, Ophelia's grave in *Hamlet*. The type providing the most potential for a spectacular entrance is a 'star-trap', which has a sort of spring-loaded trampoline below it, and door 'leaves' arranged like a star which are supposed to spring open just as your head rockets up from beneath. Not for the faint-hearted actor

turn over   instruction from the first assistant director on a film unit to start the film stock running through the camera when the director is ready to shoot. The operator will shout 'speed!' when the film is at full speed and the lens is focused ready for the shot

Variety   shows made up of a mix of musical acts, circus-type acts and 'comic turns'; much of this sort of work has been either absorbed or stifled by television

Vaudeville   roughly, the American term for what Brits call, or called, Variety

wardrobe   clothes worn onstage are always part of either the company's or the actor's own 'wardrobe'. The person in charge of costumes is always the Wardobe Mistress (or Master)

West End   geographically, the area of London bordered by (roughly) the Strand, Shaftesbury Avenue and Oxford Street. The West End theatres are the London showcases for Britain's commercial producers, in the same way as Broadway is for American producers in New York

USEFUL CONTACTS

Youth theatre

United Kingdom

National Association of
 Youth Theatres
The Custard Factory
Gibb Street
Birmingham B9 4AA
Tel: 0121 608 2111

National Youth Theatre of
 Great Britain
443 Holloway Road
London N7 6LW
Tel: 0171 281 3863
web site at http://www.ucl.ac.uk./
 BloomsburyTheatre/nyt.htm

Producer, Youth Theatre Events
Education Department
The Royal National Theatre
London SE1 9PX
Tel: 0171 452 3312

Youth Theatre in Wales:
Contact Pauline Crossley on
 01222 265033
e-mail: p.crossley@wlec.co.uk

Youth Theatre in Scotland:
Education Officer
Royal Lyceum Theatre
Edinburgh EH3 9AX
Tel: 0131 229 7404

United States

American Alliance for Theatre and
 Education
Arizona State University College
 of Fine Arts
Tel: (602) 965 6064

Australia

Carclew Youth Arts Centre
11 Jeffcott Street
North Adelaide
SA 5006
Tel: (08) 6267 5111
Fax: (08) 8239 0689

Amateur theatre

International Theatre Institute
4 St George's House
Hanover Square
London W1R 9AJ
UK
Tel: 0171 491 0072

United Kingdom

The Central Council for Amateur
  Theatre
5 Rye Hill Road
Harlow
Essex
Tel: 01279 423821

The England Drama Association
11 Howard Road
Birmingham B25 8AL
Tel: 0121 707 6684

Drama Association of Wales*
The Library
Singleton Road
Cardiff CF2 2ET
Tel: 01222 452200
Fax: 01222 452277

*N.B. The Drama Association of
Wales has a substantial library of
playscripts in sets which can be
borrowed. To take advantage of
this, your theatre company will
have to join the library and pay an
annual subscription. Membership is
not restricted to British groups – the
library has members in Europe and
in North America. Phone or fax for
details.

Scottish Community Drama
  Association
5 York Place
Edinburgh EH1 3EB
Tel: 0131 557 5552

Little Theatre Guild of Great
  Britain
12 Waldegrave Court
Teddington
TW11 8LS
Tel: 01892 534710

International Amateur Theatre
  Association
c/o Ernst and Young
Rolls House
7 Rolls Buildings
Fetter Lane
London EC4 1NH
Tel: (Secretary) 01472 343424
      (Chairman) 01708 450816

National Drama Festivals
  Association
24 Jubilee Road
Formby
Liverpool
Tel: 01704 872421

The Edinburgh Fringe Festival
180 High Street
Edinburgh
EH1 1QS
Tel: 0131 226 5257
Fax: 0131 220 4205
e-mail: admin@edfringe.com

North America

National Centre:
Theatre USA
1008 Ferdinand
Detroit
MI 48209
USA
Tel: (313) 843 6940
Fax: (313) 221 1734

Theatre Canada
146 Memorial Drive
Gander
Newfoundland A1V 1A8
Tel: (709) 256 3796
Fax: (709) 256 3796

Australia

The Mustardseed Project
GPO Box 1981
Canberra ACT 2601
Tel: (61) 624 80811
Fax: (61) 624 76829

Playscripts, licensing, etc

Samuel French Ltd
53 Fitzroy Street
London W1P 6JR
UK
Tel: 0171 387 9373
Fax: 0171 387 2161

Samuel French, Inc
45 West 25th Street
New York
NY 10010
USA
Tel: (212) 206 8990

Samuel French, Inc
7623 Sunset Boulevard
Hollywood
CA 90046
USA
Tel: (213) 876 0570

Samuel French (Canada) Ltd
80 Richmond Street East
Toronto
Ontario M5C 1P1
Canada
Tel: (416) 363 3536

Dominie (agents for Samuel
    French Ltd)
8 Cross Street
Brookvale
New South Wales 2100
Australia
Tel: 612 9905 0201

Children's theatre

ASSITEJ
(International Association for
  Theatre for Young People)
Polka Theatre for Children
240 The Broadway
Wimbledon
London SW19 1SB
UK
Tel: 0181 542 4258
Fax: 0181 542 7723

The Creative Arts Team
New York University
715 Broadway
New York
NY 10003
Tel: (212) 998 5272

Carclew Youth Arts Centre
11 Jeffcott Street
North Adelaide
SA 5006
Australia
Tel: (08) 6267 5111
Fax: (08) 8239 0689

Puppet Centre Trust
Battersea Arts Centre
London SW11 5TN
UK
Tel: 0171 228 5335
Fax: 0171 978 5207

Union Internationale de la
  Marionette
Cross Border Arts
Peterborough Arts Centre
Peterborough PE2 5JQ
UK

Ecole de Jacques Lecoq
57 Rue de Faubourg St Denis
78010 Paris
France
Tel: (1) 4770 4478

Theatre Centre Young People's
  Theatre Company
(National Touring)
Toynbee Workshops
3 Gunthorpe Street
London
E1 7RQ
Tel: 0171 377 0379
Fax: 0171 377 1376

Theatre in Education

United Kingdom

National Drama
4 Hollin Drive
Leeds LS16 5NE

London Drama
Holborn Centre for the Performing
  Arts
Three Cups Yard
Sandland Street
London WC1R 4PZ
Tel/fax: 0171 405 4519

Education Department
Royal National Theatre
London SE1 9PX
Tel: 0171 452 3333

Central School of Speech and
  Drama
64 Eton Avenue
London NW3 3HY
Tel: 0171 722 8183
Fax: 0171 722 4132

United States

American Alliance for Theatre and
  Education
Arizona State University
PO Box 872002
Tempe AZ 85287-2002
Tel: (602) 965 5359
Fax: (602) 965 5351

School of Education
(Department of Music and
  Performing Arts Professions)
New York University
Pless Annex 23
82 Washington Square East
New York
NY 10003-6680
Tel: (212) 998 5868
Fax: (212) 995 4569

Australia

Educational Drama Association
  of NSW
Joint Council Block B
Leichardt
New South Wales
Tel: (02) 9560 4966
Fax: (02) 9560 4070

Drama and therapy

Institute of Dramatherapy
Roehampton Institute
University of Surrey
London
UK
Tel: 0181 392 3000
Fax: 0181 392 3273
http://www.roehampton.ac.uk./
  academic/arts&hum/drama/drath.
  html

National Association of Drama
  Therapy
15245 Shady Grove Road
Suite 130
Rockville MD 20850
USA
Tel: (301) 258 9210
Fax: (301) 990 9771

Summer schools and pre-training courses

United Kingdom

Many of the Conference of Drama Schools colleges now offer Access and Summer courses as 'pre-training training'. I suggest you enquire at any of the schools in the CDS list, which appears on pages 143–5.

Training for teenage students who may wish to go on to full-time drama training later:

BRIT Performing Arts and
  Technology School
60 The Crescent
Croydon CR0 2HN
Tel: 0181 665 5242
Fax: 0181 665 5197

Arts Educational School
Tring Park
Tring HP23 5LX
Tel: 01442 824255

The Education Department at the Royal National Theatre and the National Youth Theatre both offer summer courses for young people with a passion for acting. Contact the RNT on 0171 452 3333 and NYT on 0171 281 3863.

Evening and weekend courses are run by:
The Questors Theatre
12 Mattock Lane
London W5 5BQ
Tel: 0181 567 0011

Australia

The St Laurence Arts Centre
505 Pitt Street
Sydney NSW 2000
Tel: (02) 9212 6000
Fax: (02) 9281 3964
Offers Access courses.

For summer courses in Australia and New Zealand, once again the best source of information is probably *Lowdown* magazine, tel: (08) 8267 5111 or Fax: (08) 8239 0689.

United States

The following organization publishes both a Directory of Theater Training Programs and a Summer Theater Directory:

American Theater Works Inc
Theater Directories
PO Box 519
Dorset
Vermont 05251
Tel: (802) 867 2223

Training in North America

A comprehensive guide is the *Directory of Theater Training Programs* published by American Theater Works Inc
Dorset, Vermont 05251
USA
Tel: (802) 867 2223
or available from:
The Drama Bookshop
723 Seventh Avenue
New York
NY 10019
USA
Tel: (212) 944 0595

In Canada, contact:
350 Albert Street
Suite 600
Ottawa KIR 1B1
Tel: (613) 563 1236
Fax: (613) 563 9745

National Theatre School of Canada
 (Ecole Nationale)
5030 St Denis
Montreal
Quebec H2J 2L8
Tel: (514) 842 7954
Fax: (514) 842 5661

Disability issues:
Association for Theatre and
 Disability
300 UCLA Medical Plaza
Los Angeles
CA 90095 6967

Training for Americans in Europe:

Theater Department
Stephen F. Austin State University
1936 North Street
Nacogdoches
Texas 75962-9090
USA
Tel: (409) 468 4003
Fax: (409) 468 1168

Department of Drama
College of Fine Arts 106
Carnegie-Mellon University
Pittsburgh
PA 15213
USA
Tel: (412) 268 2392

British American Drama Academy
900 West End Avenue ISF
New York
NY 10025
Tel/fax: (212) 749 0120

Training in Australia and New Zealand

Directions – a comprehensive
contact guide to training for the
performing arts in Australia and
New Zealand, published by:
Lowdown Magazine
11 Jeffcott Street
North Adelaide SA5006
Australia
Tel: (08) 8267 5111
Fax: (08) 8239 0689

The Australia Council
181 Lawson Street
Redfern
Sydney, Australia
Tel: (612) 9950 9000

National Academy of Singing and
Dramatic Art
PO Box 22–772
Christchurch, New Zealand
Tel: 64 3 379 9461

Disability Issues:
Arts Access
South bank 3006
Victoria, Australia
Tel: (613) 969 98299

D.A.D.A.A.
PO Box 1080
Fremantle WA 6160
Australia
Tel: (618) 9430 6616

Training in the United Kingdom

Conference of UK Drama Schools

Arts Educational London Schools
14 Bath Road W4 1LY
Tel: 0181 994 9366
Fax: 0181 994 9274

Birmingham School of Speech &
  Drama
45 Church Rd
Edgbaston
Birmingham B15 3SW
Tel: 0121 454 3424
Fax: 0121 456 4496

Bristol Old Vic Theatre School
2 Downside Road
Clifton
Bristol BS8 2XF
Tel: 0117 973 3535
Fax: 0117 923 9371

Central School of Speech & Drama
Embassy Theatre
64 Eton Avenue
Swiss Cottage NW3 3HY
Tel: 0171 722 8183

Cygnet Training Theatre
New Theatre Friars Gate
Exeter EX2 4AZ
Tel/fax: 01392 277189

Drama Centre London
176 Prince of Wales Road
NW5 3PT
Tel: 0171 267 1177
Fax: 0171 485 7129

East 15 Acting School
Hatfields & Corbett Theatre
Rectory Lane
Loughton
Essex IG10 3RU
Tel: 0181 508 5983
Fax: 0181 508 7521

East 15 Acting School
Sheriff Hutton Park
Sheriff Hutton
York YO6 1RH
Tel/fax: 01347 878442

GSA Guildford School of Acting
Millmead Terrace
Guildford
Surrey GU2 5AT
Tel: 01483 560701

Guildhall School of Music & Drama
Silk Street
Barbican EC2Y 8DT
Tel: 0171 628 2571
Fax: 0171 256 9438

LAMDA
Tower House
226 Cromwell Road
SW5 0SR
Tel: 0171 373 9883

Manchester Metropolitan
  University School of Theatre
The Capitol Building
School Lane
Didsbury
Manchester M20 0HT
Tel: 0161 247 2000 Ext 7123
Fax: 0161 448 0135

Mountview Theatre School
104 Crouch Hill N8 9EA
Tel: 0181 340 5885
Fax: 0181 348 1727

The Oxford School of Drama
Sansomes Farm Studios
Woodstock
Oxford OX20 1ER
Tel: 01993 812883
Fax: 01993 811220

Queen Margaret College
Clerwood Terrace
Edinburgh EH12 8TS
Tel: 0131 317 3542

Rose Bruford College
Lamorbey Park
Burnt Oak Lane
Sidcup
Kent DA15 9DF
Tel: 0181 300 3024
Fax: 0181 308 0542

Royal Academy of Dramatic Art
18–22 Chenies Street
WC1E 7EX
Tel: 0171 636 7076
Fax: 0171 323 3865

Royal Scottish Academy of Music
  and Drama
100 Renfrew Street
Glasgow G2 3DB
Tel: 0141 332 4101

Webber Douglas Academy of
  Dramatic Art
30 Clareville St SW7 5AP
Tel: 0171 370 4154
Fax: 0171 373 5639

Welsh College of Music and
  Drama
School of Drama Castle Grounds
Cathays Park
Cardiff CF1 3ER
Tel: 01222 371440

The Conference of Drama Schools
publishes a UK Guide to Drama
Training available from:
Westlake Publishing Ltd
17 Sturton Street
Cambridge CB1 2SN
Tel: 01223 566763
Fax: 01223 566945

You can also access information on
the Internet about British drama
schools at http://www.drama.ac.uk

National Council for Drama
  Training
5 Tavistock Place
London WC1H 9SS
Tel: 0171 387 3650

Information regarding disabilities:
Artsline
54 Chalton Street
London NW1 1HS
Tel: 0171 388 2227

GRAEAE Theatre Company
Interchange Studios
Dalby Street
London
NW5 3NQ
Tel: 0171 267 1959
Fax: 0171 267 2703

The Richard Attenborough
  Centre for Disability and the Arts
University of Leicester
PO Box 138
Leicester LE1 9HN
Tel: 0116 252 2455

Professional organizations and publications

United Kingdom

The Actors' Centre
1a Tower Street
London WC2H 9NP
Tel: 0171 240 3896

The Actors' Handbook
Bloomsbury Publishing
2 Soho Square
London WC1V 6HB
Tel: 0171 494 2111

British Equity
Guild House
Upper St Martins Lane
London WC2H 9EG
Tel: 0171 379 6000
Fax: 0171 379 7001

The London Fringe (monthly
  magazine)
PO Box 338
St Albans
Herts AL1 1AL
Tel: 01727 821141

Professional Casting Report
PO Box 100
Broadstairs
Kent CT10 1UJ
Tel: 01843 860885

*The Spotlight**
(Publishers, *Contacts*)
7 Leicester Place
London WC2H 7BP
Tel: 0171 437 7631
Fax: 0171 437 5881

The Stage Newspaper Ltd (weekly)
47 Bermondsey Street
London SE1 3XT
Tel: 0171 403 1818
Fax: 0171 403 1418
www.thestage.co.uk

*Please note that there is a separate
casting directory published in the
Irish Republic:
Stagecast
15 Eaton Square
Monkstown, Dublin
Tel: 3531 2808968

North America

American Federation of TV &
  Radio Artists (AFTRA)
260 Madison Avenue
New York NY 10016
Tel: (212) 532 0800

*The Back Stage Handbook for
  Performing Artists*
BPI Bookstore
1515 Broadway
New York, NY 10036
Also publishers of *Back Stage*
  (weekly newspaper).
Back Stage now available on
  http://www.backstage.com
(This service also has an interactive
element, which allows you access
to all the casting notices which
have been published recently in
Back Stage and *Back Stage West*.)

Henderson Guides (information re
  agents, casting directors, etc.)
The Drama Bookshop
723 7th Avenue
2nd Floor @ 48th Street
NY 10036
Tel: (212) 944 0595
Fax: (212) 730 8739

The Players' Guide
164 West 64th Street
Suite 1305
New York, NY 10036
Tel: (212) 869 3570

The American Equity
165 West 46th Street
New York
NY 10036
Tel: (212) 944 1030
Fax: (212) 719 9815

Screen Actors Guild (SAG)
1515 Broadway
44th Floor
New York 10036
Tel: (212) 944 1030
Fax: (212) 944 6774

A.C.T.R.A
223q Yonge Street
Toronto
Ontario
Canada N43 28S
Tel: (416) 489 1311

The Actors' Centre
12 West 27th Street
Suite 1700
New York, NY 10001
Tel: (212) 447 6309
Fax: (212) 447 9688

Australia

The Australian Casting Directory
PO Box 2001
Leumeah NSW
Australia 2560
Tel: 46 28 6365
Fax: 46 28 6367

Australian Equity
PO Box 723
Strawberry Hill
NSW 2012
Australia
Tel: (02) 9333 0999
Fax: (02) 9333 0933

Stage Whispers
PO Box 318
Monbulk
Victoria 3793
Australia
Tel: (03) 9752 1065

The Actors' Centre
241 Devonshire Street
Surry Hills
New South Wales 2010
Australia
Tel: (02) 9310 4077
Fax: (02) 9310 2891

New Zealand Equity
Tel: (649) 355 1850
Fax: (649) 355 1855

INDEX